SOUT
WA

32 downland rambles from Brighton, Worthing and surrounding district

First published 1981
Reprinted 1982
Second edition 1986
Third edition 1989
Reprinted 1991

COLIN ULPH · SHOREHAM BY SEA

While every care has been taken in the compilation of this book, the author cannot accept responsibility for inaccuracies due to such factors as removal of gates and stiles or the ploughing of paths. All of the routes use either public rights of way or other paths over which the public has undisputed access. Please report any obstruction to the highway authority so that the way may be cleared for others. Some of the routes will be affected by the construction of the proposed Brighton bypass, so take care to follow signposted diversions.

At the time of publication all starting places are on or near bus routes, but details should be checked when planning your walk. All car parking is entirely at the owner's risk, even where permission has been given to use a private car park.

Ordnance Survey maps covering the routes:
1:50000 Sheet 197 — Walks 1-3
Sheet 198 — Walks 3-32
1:25000 Outdoor Leisure Map: Brighton and Sussex Vale — Walks 17-29

BRITISH LIBRARY CATALOGUING IN PUBLICATION DATA

Ulph, Colin
Southdown walks: 32 downland rambles from Brighton and Worthing. — 3rd ed.
1. Walking — England — South Downs — Guide-books
2. South Downs (England) — Description and travel — Guide-books
I. Title
796.5'1'094226 DA670.S98

ISBN 0 9511088 1 6

Colin Ulph, Coombes, 281 Upper Shoreham Road, Shoreham by Sea, West Sussex BN43 6BB

Typeset by Blackmore Typesetting Services, Hove
Produced by Kensett Ltd., Hove

THE ROUTES

PREFACE TO THE FIRST EDITION

Those of us who live in the busy coastal towns of central Sussex are fortunate indeed in having the South Downs right on our doorstep. Not only because they protect us from the worst of the winter weather and prevent our towns from uncontrolled expansion to the north, but also because they offer the opportunity to enjoy invigorating walks in delightful surroundings.

The northern aspect of tree-crowned Chanctonbury and the Wealden panorama from Dyke Hill are familiar enough, even to those who observe the countryside from the discomfort of a car. Yet it is true to say that no-one can claim knowledge of the real charm of our lovely downs without leaving motor transport behind and setting out to explore them on foot. Countless traces of prehistoric civilisation; scores of ancient grey churches; cosy country pubs; the unique flora and fauna of chalk hills; the graceful contours of the downs themselves; fresh, clean air; and a peace and spaciousness which is almost incredible only a mile or two from the congested coastline: all these delights and more await the downland explorer.

This book aims to be your companion and guide to some of the most picturesque paths on the Sussex downs, including many sections of that famed long-distance route, the South Downs Way. I hope that its use will stimulate both a quest for further knowledge of our local history and countryside and a desire to venture forth on more of the hundreds of tracks with which the downs are interlaced, so helping to ensure that they remain open for the recreation of future generations.

I suggest that on your rambles you take a compass and a detailed Ordnance Survey map to assist in identifying the views, a camera to capture the enjoyment of the day, some waterproof and sturdy footwear to combat the notorious Sussex mud, and above all, your TIME, to savour to the full the magic of the downs.

May you gain as much pleasure from the use of this book as I and my family have in its preparation.

COLIN ULPH
April 1981

PREFACE TO THE THIRD EDITION

The success of the first *Southdown Walks* encouraged me to produce in 1986 a second edition, enlarged to include many new rambles, as well as old favourites which I had rewalked and updated.

This third edition comprises the same routes, which are still valid and passable, with the possible exception of temporary diversions where fallen trees have not been cleared after the 1987 "hurricane". Although I have not changed the text, you will notice also that tree-crowned summits like Lancing Clump, Highdown and Chanctonbury Ring are looking a bit threadbare since that unforgettable October night.

However, the effects of the hurricane will be nothing compared to those of the long-threatened Brighton bypass, which will cause the permanent closure or diversion of some of our best-loved paths and the obstruction of countless views by high embankments blocking off the valleys. This dreaded "concrete collar" is expected to gradually encircle the built-up area from Shoreham to Stanmer Park in stages over the next five or six years, so watch out for diversions affecting Walks 18-22 and 25, once the work gets under way.

Let us hope that a glimpse of the destruction wrought by one multi-million pound road scheme will consolidate opposition to a similar mistake north of Worthing, where the picturesque and historic Cissbury area must be protected at all costs.

I trust that this little book will continue to play its part in encouraging a love of the downs, and determination to use the paths, preserve the views and conserve the wildlife which make them so special.

March 1989

SELECTING A WALK

The routes in this book cater for a wide variety of tastes. To help in selecting a walk, here is a list of the features to be found in some of them.

Longer walks (9-16 miles)	**1, 2, 9, 10, 11, 15, 19, 21, 26, 29, 31**
Shorter walks (3-5½ miles)	**3, 4, 6, 8, 17, 18, 20, 23, 27, 28**
Climbs 1000 feet or more	**1, 9, 19, 24, 26, 31**
Climbs 300 feet or less	**3, 6, 11, 17, 18**
South Downs Way	**1, 4, 5, 7, 9, 10, 12, 13, 16, 19, 23, 24, 25, 26, 29, 31**
Downs Link	**9, 11**
Riverbanks	**2, 11, 12, 14, 15, 16, 17**
Woodland sections	**1, 2, 3, 4, 8, 10, 23, 24, 26, 27, 28**
Disused railway tracks	**9, 11, 12, 17, 22**
Ancient churches	**2, 3, 4, 5, 9, 10, 12, 13, 14, 15, 17, 20, 21, 22, 23, 24, 25, 26, 28, 29, 30, 31, 32**
Watermills	**11, 23**
Windmills	**6, 10, 25, 30, 31**
Castles	**2, 9, 31**
Hillforts	**3, 7, 8, 10, 19, 22, 23, 24, 26, 27**
Ponds and lakes	**1, 2, 3, 7, 10, 11, 17, 21, 24, 26, 28**
Seaside	**30, 32**
Inns at about half-way	**3, 9, 10, 11, 15, 17, 19, 21, 22, 23, 25, 26, 28, 29, 30, 31**

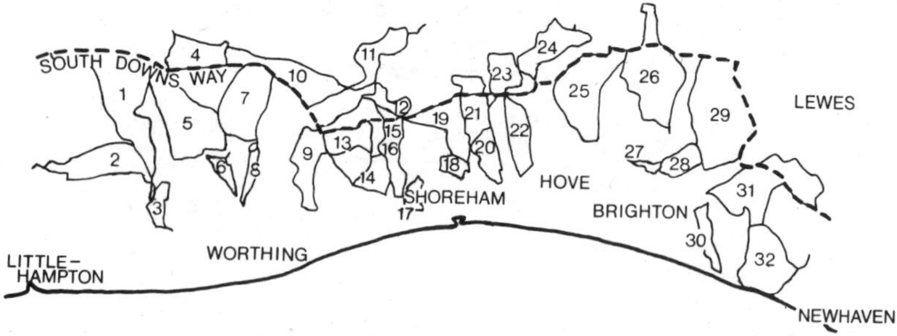

Walk 1

AMBERLEY MOUNT

Patching Pond — Patching — Michelgrove — Harrow Hill — Chantry Hill — Kithurst Hill — Rackham Hill — Amberley Mount — Wepham Down — Barpham Hill — Patching Hill — Patching — Patching Pond

Distance 16 mls **Climbing** 1020 ft **Highest point** 700 ft

Starting point The layby at Patching Pond, on the north side of the A27 Worthing-Arundel road, next to the Horse and Groom public house (map reference TQ 087056).

A most enjoyable day's ramble along well-used paths and gentle gradients. The route incorporates many panoramic views and a popular stretch of the South Downs Way. The woodland section just before Patching Hill can be muddy after wet weather, but the worst parts can be avoided without much trouble.

Start along the footpath which leaves the road immediately west of the pond. In 50 yards cross a stile and continue north along the L side of a meadow. At its north-west corner cross another stile and skirt the south and west sides of a large field. Just before the red brick houses go L and emerge on a lane; turn L and in 150 yards go R at the junction, passing the lane leading to Patching church. Walk on up the road until it ends at a large, wooden gate.

WALKS 1 AND 2 DIVERGE HERE

After passing through the gate take the R fork to continue your northward route along a footpath which soon descends with a reservoir mound L. At a crosspaths in the middle of a field go straight on, and in 200 yards cross a stile into a small wood. Soon you will arrive at a poultry farm. Turn L along the lane here, and remain on it for the next 2½ miles, through some truly unspoiled Sussex countryside. You will pass a curious pair of houses like bookends on either side of the lane, the large estate of Michelgrove — said to have been visited by Henry VIII in a more prosperous heyday — and the

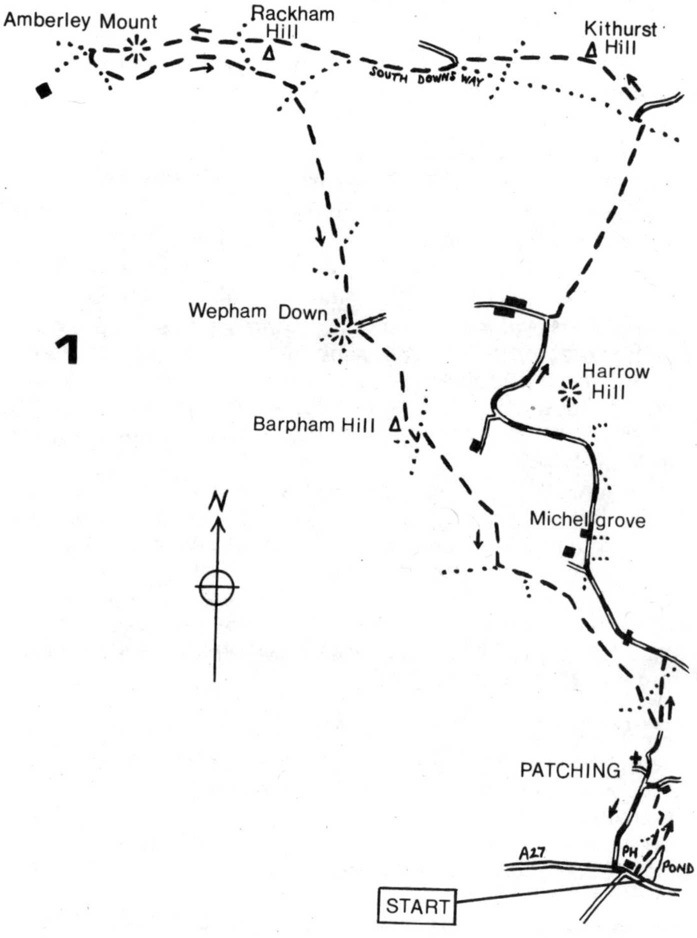
Amberley Mount
Rackham Hill
Kithurst Hill
SOUTH DOWNS WAY
Wepham Down
1
Harrow Hill
Barpham Hill
N
Michel grove
PATCHING
A27
PH
POND
START

base of Harrow Hill, the site of Neolithic flint mines and an Iron Age hillfort.

When the lane is about to turn L towards Lee Farm, take a chalky track R and in a few yards resume your northerly direction. Now the South Downs Way beckons, and you reach it after 1¼ miles, at the car park on Chantry Hill. Next go down the tarmac road for about 100 yards, and after a sharp R bend find the bridleway L which in a further ½ mile will take you to the trig point at the top of Kithurst Hill, at 700 feet the highest point on the walk.

Chanctonbury Ring is prominent in the east, while to the south there is a succession of downland summits to attract the gaze. From L to R they are Cissbury Ring, Church Hill, Blackpatch Hill, Highdown, Harrow Hill, Barpham Hill and Wepham Down. The view north to Storrington is obscured by trees, but beyond the town a view extends across the Weald to the sandy ridges of north Sussex and Surrey.

Continue to walk west, and within a mile rejoin the South Downs Way at another parking area. Follow the Way through a clump of trees and find the next triangulation pillar marking the top of Rackham Hill, at 634 feet. Now you can see Amberley Mount just a mile ahead, with the Arun valley and the downs beyond on the L, and Amberley village and the Wild Brooks to the R. Pass over the summit of the Mount, noting the distant prospect of Arundel Castle to the south, and a superb view of the western downs and the Sussex Weald.

Descend along the Way for about 300 yards, and just before a large farm go L to pick up a chalky track which doubles back around the south side of Amberley Mount. In 200 yards take the L fork, to stay close to the ridge top, and on reaching the start of a conifer plantation go through a gate L to resume your eastward route with the trees just L. Soon this path becomes a grassy bridleway between hedges. At a T-junction where the tree clump east of Rackham Hill appears ½ mile ahead go R and in 20 yards take a L turn. You are now on a bridleway which you must follow for the next 1¾ miles as you head south, at first between hedgerows and later across open downland.

The path climbs at length to the top of Wepham Down, and here you take a L fork to head south-east uphill towards the summit of Barpham Hill (464 feet) which you reach in a further ¾ mile after passing through another clump of trees. The trig point on Barpham Hill offers the best all round view of all, including nearly all of the landmarks over which you passed earlier in the day.

Continue to walk south-east for ¼ mile. Then turn L at a crosspaths and in 20 yards go R downhill, to find a bridleway which traverses the north-east slope of the hill above Lower Barpham Farm. In about ½ mile this terraced path will bring you to an iron gate which you must go through and continue beside a field into Patching woods. Pursue your southward direction until you come to a T-junction, where you go L to walk east. In ¼ mile take a L fork, and thereafter go straight on for a further ½ mile, ignoring all paths leaving to L and R. If the going is muddy in this section, it may be best to pick your way through the woods beside the path, but be careful not to lose sight of it.

Leave the Forestry Commission woodland by a large gate, and make your way across short turf, still south-easterly, keeping a hedge on your R. Just north of Patching church you will find the gate leading on to the made-up road, and this will bring you in 1 mile to the main road near the Horse and Groom, close to Patching Pond.

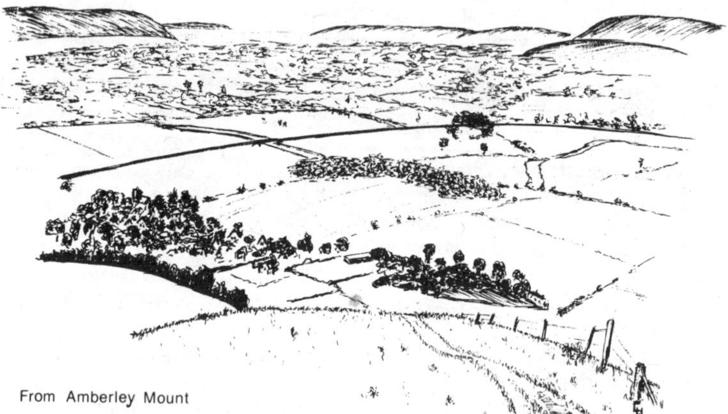

From Amberley Mount

Walk 2

BY WOODLAND TO THE ARUN

Patching Pond — Patching — Patching Hill — Patching Wood — Wepham Wood — Warningcamp — Blakehurst Farm — Patching — Patching Pond

Distance 12½ mls **Climbing** 550 ft **Highest point** 350 ft

Starting point The layby at Patching Pond, on the north side of the A27 Worthing-Arundel road, next to the Horse and Groom public house (map reference TQ 087056).

The ideal walk for days which are either hot or windy, for the extensive beechwoods between Patching and the Arun afford ample shade and shelter, on a leisurely stroll to enjoy the picturesque view across the river to Arundel Castle. Parts of the woodland walk may be muddy after wet weather, but can be avoided by taking a parallel route through the trees.

Follow Walk 1 as far as the gate at the end of the lane through Patching. After closing the gate behind you take the L fork, uphill into a field. As you go, tree-capped Highdown appears to the south, while to your R unfolds a panoramic view to that more celebrated crown of beeches at Chanctonbury Ring, between the nearer hills of Blackpatch and Cissbury. Keep this view R until you enter the woods through another gate. Now press on north-west for a further ½ mile, and then westward, along a sometimes muddy track, ignoring all turns to L and R.

Soon the bridleway becomes more distinct, and in a further mile crosses a lane at a red brick cottage L to continue the westward direction as a farm track. In another mile you will arrive in a small clearing where 5 paths converge: bear R through a gate and then take a narrow bridleway R which descends steeply through the woods. Emerging in a valley, take a L turn and in 200 yards fork R to walk through the valley bottom. In just over ¼ mile follow the bridleway as it climbs a little on the L side of the valley and enters another small wood,

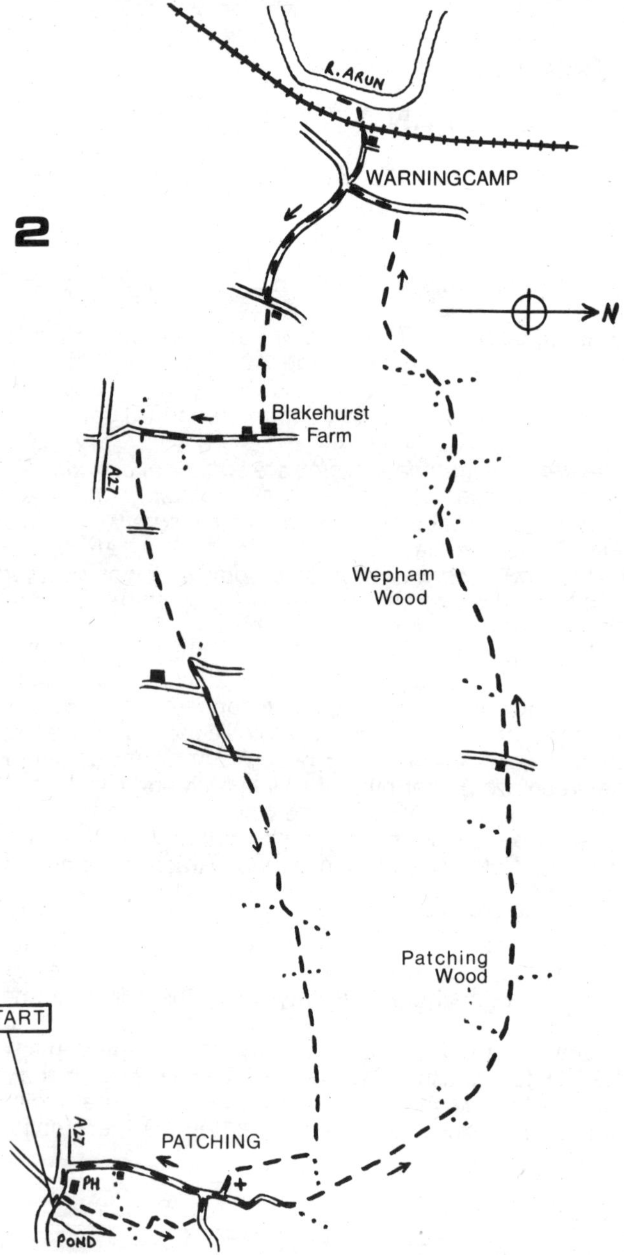
R. ARUN
WARNINGCAMP
2
N
Blakehurst
Farm
A27
Wepham
Wood
Patching
Wood
START
A27
PATCHING
PH
POND

passing through it at about 100 feet above the valley floor.

On reaching a road walk L along it into the hamlet of Warningcamp, and at the crossroads go R. At the end of the lane cross the railway with great care, and make for the riverbank where you will want to pause to admire a delightful view across the Arun to historic Arundel Castle, seat of the Dukes of Norfolk. Notice its ancient keep on the mound to the R and the Roman Catholic cathedral L.

Now it is time to turn back. Retrace your steps across the railway and up the lane to Warningcamp. This time go straight on at the crossroads, past some picturesque cottages and later between hedgerows as far as a T-junction. Turn L for a few yards and then find a footpath R, just south of Norfolk Cottages. Walk east for ½ mile and emerge on a lane at Blakehurst Farm. Here turn R, walk down the lane for a further ½ mile and then take a bridleway L into the woods. Go east for just under a mile, crossing a track on the way, until you come to another lane at a hairpin bend. Go straight on (the southern arm of the bend), observing Priorsdean Farm across the field R.

At the next bend pass through a large gate and continue east long a surfaced bridleway. After ¼ mile cross a north-south lane to take the rough track through the woods. Just after another large gate this bears L, but in 100 yards you must take a R turn to resume your eastward trek. In just under 1 mile you will emerge from the wood on a path between fields with a view to Patching church and Highdown R. After 400 yards cross a stile R and take the footpath which will take you south to a farmyard, and then to the church of St John the Divine.

Patching church dates almost entirely from the 13th century, the exceptions being the shingled spire and the vestry, which were added at the time of a substantial restoration in the 19th century. The interior is dark, as all of the narrow, lancet windows are filled with stained glass, but there are some fine arches and a 15th century octagonal font.

To regain your starting point walk south through the village for 1 mile, and turn L on reaching the main road.

3

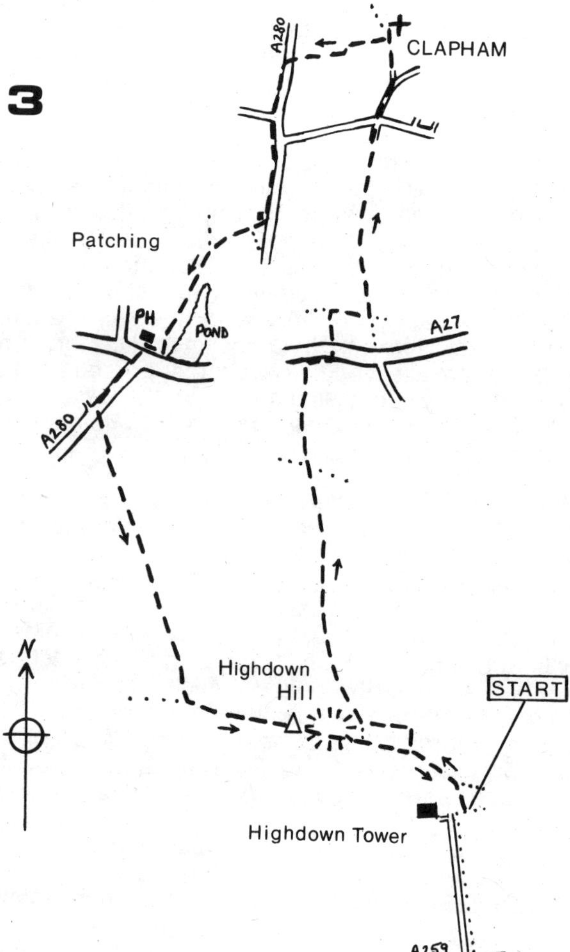
CLAPHAM
A280
Patching
PH
POND
A27
A280
N
Highdown
Hill
START
Highdown Tower
A259

Walk 3
CLAPHAM AND HIGHDOWN

Highdown Tower — Clapham — Patching Pond — Highdown Hill — Highdown Tower

Distance 5 mls **Climbing** 290 ft **Highest point** 266 ft

Starting point The car park just east of Highdown Tower, a prominent house with public gardens specialising in chalk flora. It is approached by a narrow lane leading north from the A259 between Goring and Ferring. Map reference TQ 099041.

A straightforward little ramble of gentle slopes and plenty of variety, including leafy woods, open downs and a solid, Early English, flint church.

Leave the car park at its northern side and pick up a track leading L across the down behind Highdown Tower. Pass the curious Miller's Tomb L, the final resting place of John Oliver, the mad miller of Highdown Mill in the 18th century, who (so the story goes) built his tomb before his death and ordered that he should be buried upside down so that his feet would be ready for their walk to heaven.

Continue along the path which skirts the north edge of the grassland, with a wood on your R. Shortly before arriving at the conspicuous clump of trees on the summit of Highdown Hill, find a bridleway leaving R and descend northward through the woods. Continue north when you emerge from the wood, and arrive in a further ½ mile on the Worthing — Arundel trunk road. Walk R along the roadside verge for about 100 yards until you are nearly at the dual carriageway. Then cross the road and go north on a footpath into another wood.

When a wire fence bars your northward progress take the R footpath for about 200 yards before turning L to resume the route north. Soon this leaves the wood and goes on to enter the tiny village of Clapham, where you must cross a west-east lane and follow all signs to the parish church.

The church of St Mary the Virgin, surrounded by attractive woodland, dates originally from Norman times, but most of its flint fabric is 13th century Early English with some Perpendicular windows. The interior contains some interesting monuments and brasses.

Outside the lychgate, turn L but in 20 yards, opposite a flint wall, go R along a footpath which once more enters the woods. Emerging at a stile, cross it to descend the L side of a field with a good view of Patching across the valley. Arriving at the Long Furlong road A280, turn L along it for just over ¼ mile until you get to the village hall. Cross the stile beside this and walk south-westerly across the cricket pitch. Beyond it continue in the same direction through a shallow valley and arrive at a south-north path in front of a long hedge. Here turn L to walk beside the hedge southward, with Patching Pond visible on your L. At the corner of the field cross a further stile, and in about 50 yards you will arrive back on the trunk road near the Horse and Groom public house.

Now you must cross the main road and walk south-west along the A280 Littlehampton road for about 400 yards. Then find a footpath L which first passes a small sewage works R, crosses a stile and then a short wooden footbridge across a brook. Now begin the steady climb back to the ridge which culminates in tree-crowned Highdown, along the R side of 2 large fields. Near the top of the ridge go through a small area of scrub and bear L to attain the white trig point at the summit of Highdown Hill, 266 feet above sea level.

A property of the National Trust, Highdown is crowned not only by a clump of trees; for like its larger counterpart, Chanctonbury, it boasts an Iron Age hillfort. From the trig point the western view extends along the coast past Littlehampton and Bognor Regis; when you pass south of the trees you may see the eastern coastline between Worthing and Brighton, and the white sea cliffs beyond.

Descend the hill by its eastern side, pass the Miller's Tomb R, and arrive once more in the car park. If you have time, be sure to visit the unique chalk garden originated by Col. Frederick Stern at Highdown Tower.

Walk 4

SULLINGTON

Washington — Highden Hill — Barns Farm Hill — Sullington Hill — Sullington — Rowdell — Washington

Distance 5½ mls **Climbing** 650 ft **Highest point** 675 ft

Starting point The old Worthing Road, opposite the Frankland Arms, Washington (map reference TQ 122129).

A fine 2 mile stretch of the lofty South Downs Way is followed by a superb bostal path descending the downs, and visits to 2 contrasting country churches.

Walk south along the road for 300 yards and then go over a stile L, opposite Stocks Mead. Pursue a footpath south-easterly across a field and beyond another stile into some woods. Now the path climbs steeply for a short distance through the trees, but evens out as it passes a chalk quarry R. At the quarry entrance join a broader track which in 200 yards meets the South Downs Way at right angles. Here turn R and descend westerly to the Worthing-London trunk road.

Cross the road with great care, and again pick up the Way as it makes use of Glaseby Lane, making height quickly up the east side of Highden Hill. On reaching the open downs the bridleway levels out, revealing an ever-widening panorama. Continue along the firm and distinct track, and near the top of Barns Farm Hill (675 feet), just over a mile from the trunk road, look back for a splendid view of tree-crowned Chanctonbury in the east and the long shape of Cissbury in the south-east.

Keep to the South Downs Way until you reach an iron gate R, just before a black Dutch barn L. Go through the gate to find a bostal path which describes a semicircle around a deep coombe just below the summit of Sullington Hill. As it veers north this bridleway adopts a steeper gradient and heads for the tiny , charming village of Sullington, which you will reach after about a mile's descent from the South Downs Way.

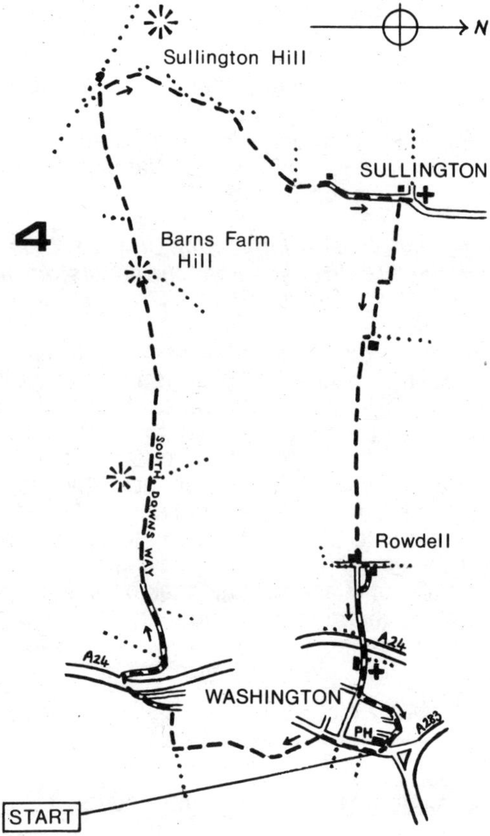
N
Sullington Hill
SULLINGTON
4
Barns Farm
Hill
SOUTH DOWNS WAY
Rowdell
A24
A24
WASHINGTON
PH
A283
START

The parish church of St Mary is a squat but appealing Early English building with Saxon work in the nave walls and Norman in the tower. Inside there is a 13th century, life-size effigy of a knight in armour, recumbent on a Saxon stone coffin. Notice also the unusual war memorial near the gate, a lamp column formed by an ancient mill-roller.

After visiting the church retrace your steps for 50 yards before taking a bridleway L opposite a large barn. The conical shape of Sullington Hill is on the southern horizon. At the end of the large field R, the path goes R a little to a gate, opening on to another field. Now continue eastward and later pass the attractive farmhouse of Barns Farm L, noting the fine view of Chanctonbury ahead.

Just after some more farm buildings do not follow the obvious lane eastward, which is not a public right of way, but go L for a few yards towards Rowdell House, and then R down a surfaced drive with attractive shrubs on either side. In due course this rejoins the lane you avoided earlier; now continue east and once more cross the trunk road, this time by a narrow road bridge. Washington church now beckons.

Also dedicated to St Mary, this sandstone church was almost completely rebuilt in 1867, but the tower dates from the 15th century. Its interior is somewhat dark, having small and heavily stained glass windows.

Shortly after passing the church, go L down School Lane, which in about ¼ mile will bring you back to your starting point.

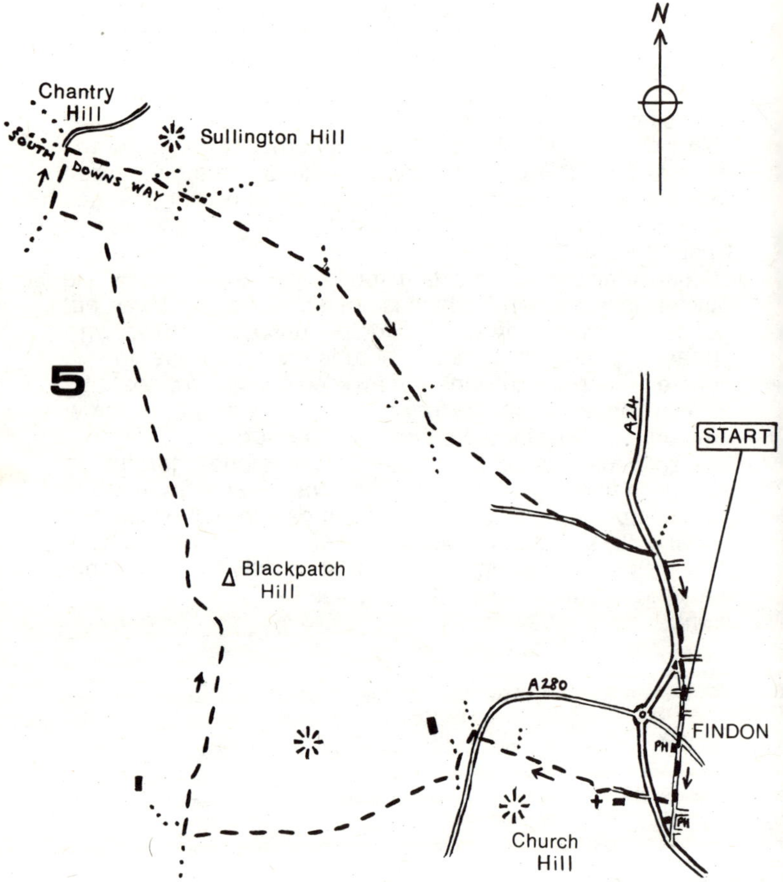

Chantry Hill
Sullington Hill
SOUTH DOWNS WAY
N
5
A24
START
Blackpatch Hill
A280
FINDON
PH
PH
Church Hill

Walk 5
CHANTRY HILL

Findon — Church Hill — Blackpatch Hill — Chantry Hill — Sullington Hill — Highden Beeches — North End — Findon

Distance 8½ mls **Climbing** 720 ft **Highest point** 650 ft

Starting point Horsham Road, Findon, in one of the laybys north of Lime Road (map reference TQ 122090).

An easy ramble with no steep hills and a superb view from Chantry Hill, above Storrington.

Walk south along Horsham Road for nearly ½ mile through Findon village, and then take the track R between Nos 56 and 58, just after Pebble Cottage. Cross the Worthing-London trunk road and continue up a lane signposted to the parish church. Pass Findon Place L, and after visiting the unusual 12th century church of St John the Baptist, with its shingled broach spire, take the track opposite the northern churchyard gate. As you go, notice a good view to the east, which comprises Chanctonbury and Cissbury Rings.

When the path reaches a R fork, go straight on up a gentle slope, keeping the cricket ground on your R. Go over a stile, and bear L uphill to arrive at the cutting made for the Long Furlong road. Cross the road to a broad track on the opposite side, but within a few yards go L at a crosspaths and then L again, keeping Tolmare Farm R. The looming hill behind the farm is Blackpatch. The bridleway goes on over a lower slope of Blackpatch. When it descends, make for the middle of a small group of beeches in the shallow valley, noting the spire of Patching church 1½ miles to the south. Continue along the same path as it climbs out of the valley, and on reaching a south-north track at the top of the ridge go R to pass just west of the top of Blackpatch (555 feet) within the next mile.

Next go through a large, metal gate and continue north, keeping a fence on your L. Stay on the higher ground as you go through a similar gate and now have the fence R. Behind you, Blackpatch takes on an almost mountainlike appearance. To the west is Harrow Hill, its summit marked by hummocks left by prehistoric miners. Shortly before the path reaches the South Downs Way it is diverted westward to join the track from Harrow Hill, and this will take you north to the motorists' viewpoint on the South Downs Way at Chantry Hill.

The downs to L and R respectively are Kithurst Hill and Sullington Hill. Beneath spreads a broad view of the Weald as far as Blackdown, the highest point in Sussex (although not on the downs), while at your feet Storrington is prominent in the foreground.

Now set off eastward along the South Downs Way close to the top of Sullington Hill (650 feet). In ½ mile take a R fork, leading behind a large, black barn, along a bridleway which skirts a wood L, known as Highden Beeches. Continue south-east in the direction of Worthing, which now appears on the sea coast. After passing the wood take the second path L, and in 100 yards go through a small gate and continue to descend through another wood. Beyond it, cross a large field diagonally towards the bulky shape of Cissbury, pass between 2 isolated tree groups, and arrive on the lane from Muntham Court. Go L, and descend to the trunk road, which you must cross once more. Next go R along a path beside the main road. After passing the fire station take the road L, leading back to Findon village.

Walk 6

SALVINGTON MILL

Findon — Roger's Farm — High Salvington — Salvington Mill — West Hill — Church Hill Shaw — Findon

Distance 4½ mls **Climbing** 300 ft **Highest point** 450 ft

Starting point On the wide approach road to Findon village, beside the Black Horse public house (map reference TQ 122083).

A short and easy ramble on the downs south-west of Findon, incorporating a visit to the recently restored post mill at High Salvington.

Cross the dual carriageway of the Worthing-London trunk road, turn L for 20 yards and then R up Roger's Lane. In just less than ½ mile, in front of the white farmhouse of Roger's Farm, walk L and 10 yards farther on follow the bridleway as it heads eastward up a gentle gradient, in the direction of the Cissbury hillfort, conspicuous across the valley. Soon the bridleway veers south, and both Chanctonbury and Cissbury Rings may now be seen on your L. After a further ¼ mile cross a road and continue to walk south, firstly along the L side of a recreation ground at the back of houses in Findon Valley, and then on a bridleway between bushes.

When the bridleway ends at an unmade road (Mill Lane) turn sharp R to walk north-west along it for more than ½ mile as it rises steadily past some truly desirable residences. On reaching Furze Road walk L for a few yards to see High Salvington windmill.

Built in the 18th century, the mill enjoyed a superb position 350 feet above sea level on the open downs. It continued to grind corn until 1897, but till the Second World War — although not in use as a mill — it was maintained in excellent repair by an owner who kept it open to the public and even served teas in the roundhouse at its base. In 1959 it came into the ownership of the Worthing Borough Council, and since 1976 a continuous programme of restoration has been in

6

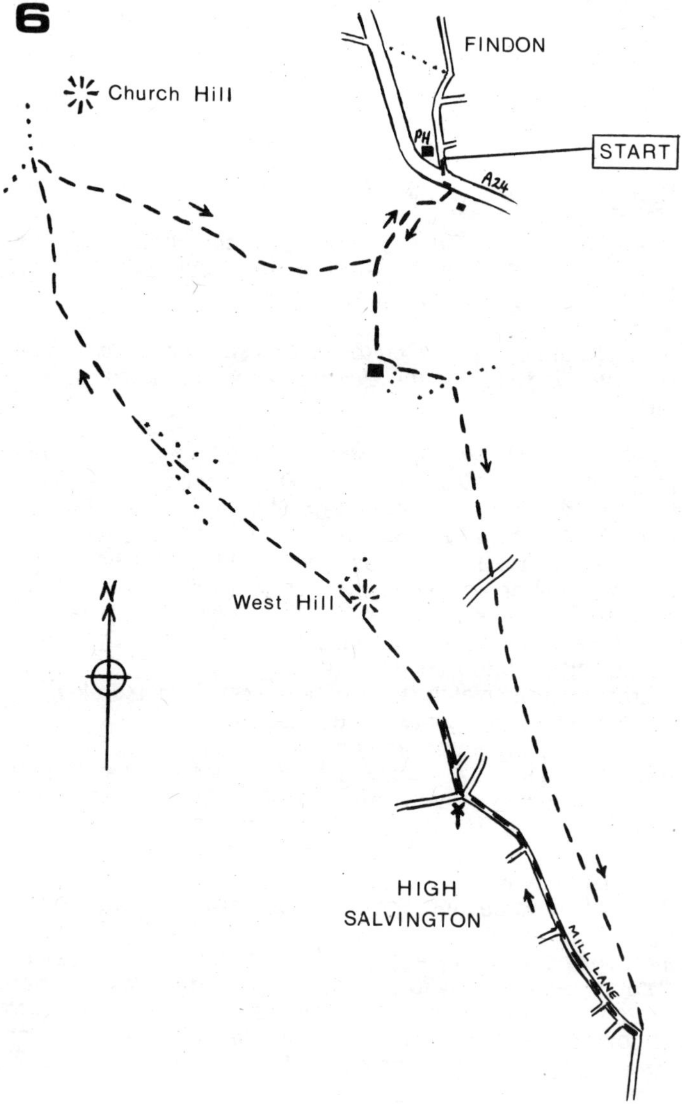
FINDON
Church Hill
PH
START
A24
West Hill
N
HIGH SALVINGTON
MILL LANE

progress. The dedicated efforts of the Friends of High Salvington Mill should help to ensure that this, one of only 2 surviving post mills in West Sussex, is preserved for posterity.

Now cross the road and walk up West Hill. When the surfaced road becomes a flinty bridleway, continue to walk north-west and observe the excellent view L to Littlehampton, Bognor Regis, and on a very clear day the spire of Chichester cathedral and the Isle of Wight downs. Pass the mast and reservoir R, and go straight on along the top of the long ridge, now with a good view R to Findon, backed by Chanctonbury Ring. Nearly ½ mile from the mast another bridleway joins your path from the L and you start to descend gently. Pass through a small wood while on the same track, and ¼ mile later turn R on a bridleway which descends eastward through the trees of Church Hill Shaw into the valley containing Roger's Farm.

Eventually you will arrive at a T-junction where Cissbury is again prominent in the east. Turn L here and arrive once more on the dual carriageway, which you must cross to arrive back at your starting point.

Salvington Windmill

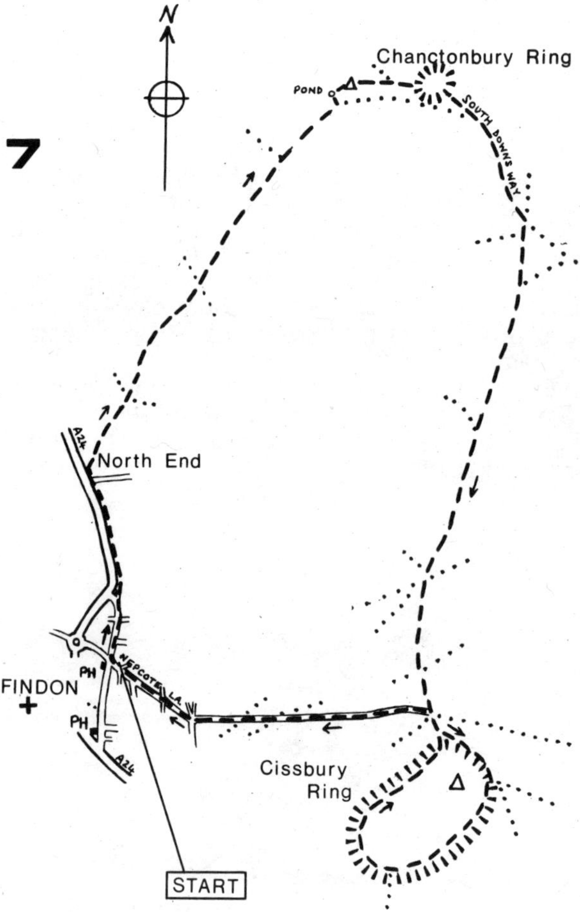
N
7
Chanctonbury Ring
POND
SOUTH DOWNS WAY
A24
North End
FINDON
PH
NEPCOTE LA.
PH
A24
Cissbury
Ring
START

Walk 7

CHANCTONBURY AND CISSBURY

Findon — North End — Chanctonbury Ring — Cissbury Ring — Nepcote Green — Findon

Distance 7½ mls **Climbing** 900 ft **Highest point** 783 ft

Starting point The layby alongside the little green in Nepcote Lane, Findon, about 50 yards from the Gun Inn (map reference TQ 123088).

The 2 Rings, prehistoric hillforts high on the Sussex downs, are both familiar landmarks and good vantage points. Here they are combined in a splendid ramble on easy gradients and firm ground.

Walk down Nepcote Lane to the Gun Inn and turn R along the village street. When this joins the Worthing-London trunk road continue northward, on the footpath running parallel with the road, but well set back from its southbound carriageway. In less than ½ mile, just after crossing the lane to Findon Park House, take a track R at North End and begin a gradual ascent between the hedgerows.

Within another ½ mile the clump of beeches on the summit of Chanctonbury comes into view in the north-east. Continue along the same path, which in 1½ miles from the main road is joined by the South Downs Way after its ascent from Washington. Near the top of the ridge there is a wooden gate across the Way. Do not go through it, but turn L to visit the dewpond.

The excellent downland dewpond, well restored and maintained by the Society of Sussex Downsmen, is a fitting foreground for the view to Chanctonbury. A stile beside it leads to the white trig point from which there is a superb all round panorama. The eastern landscape is dominated by Chanctonbury Ring, while to the south-east you may disçern the skyscrapers of Brighton and the cliffs beyond, and the tall chimneys of the Southwick power station. Cissbury Ring is ne large, long hill due south, with Worthing to its R. In the south-west the coastline falls away past Littlehampton and Bognor Regis, and on a clear day the silhouette of the Isle of Wight downs stands out on the horizon. Westward the Sussex downs stretch away to their highest point, Tegleaze, while to the north lies the vast area of woods and fields known as the Weald. Beyond this may be seen the sandy ridges around Blackdown and Leith Hill, and the chalk quarries of the North Downs, while just below your lofty vantage point the black smock mill at Rock stands above the sand quarries.

The trees of Chanctonbury, to which you must now head, were planted over 200 years ago by Charles Goring of Wiston, within an Iron Age earthwork 783 feet above sea level. This was also the site of an early British temple, excavated many years ago.

Now resume the South Downs Way as it descends to the east, passing an iron water tank, and giving a new view, eastwards to the downland range from Truleigh to Wolstonbury. After ½ mile take the bridleway R, leading south towards Cissbury. Go straight on for 2 miles, ignoring all paths to L and R, until you reach the small car park at the very foot of the Ring.

Start up the hillside, but after 100 yards bear L, to ascend the hill by the spiral path which takes you round its eastern side. Near the top, go through a small, wooden gate across the path, and turn R to attain the massive ramparts of this impressive earthwork.

Cissbury Ring, an Iron Age hillfort enclosing over 60 acres, is owned by the National Trust, which allows free access to the whole area. It was occupied even before the fort was constructed, for it was one of the foremost centres of flint mining in the Neolithic era, or Stone Age, as may be seen by the profusion of hummocks and hollows in the south-west corner of the Ring.

I recommend the walk along the top of the ramparts, which to my mind rivals that on the town walls of any medieval city. Start southward at first, by ascending the steps on the L rampart. You will notice the dome-like shape of Steep Down in the east, and as you go the flats and hotels of Worthing appear in the south, beyond the Hill Barn golf course. Rounding the south-western corner the modern development in the Findon Valley dominates the foreground, while behind it stands isolated Highdown Hill; and don't forget to look at the traces of disused flint mines on your R. Along the west wall Findon village may be seen, and soon Chanctonbury Ring appears on the northern horizon. When the Cissbury car park is immediately below, drop down the rampart, cross a stile and continue the descent to the car park.

Now take the surfaced lane L, going steadily down towards Findon. At the first road junction, in ¾ mile, ignore a turn L and continue down Nepcote Lane. Bear R at the shops, and very soon you will be back at your starting point, close to the pubs and cafes of Findon.

Chanctonbury Ring

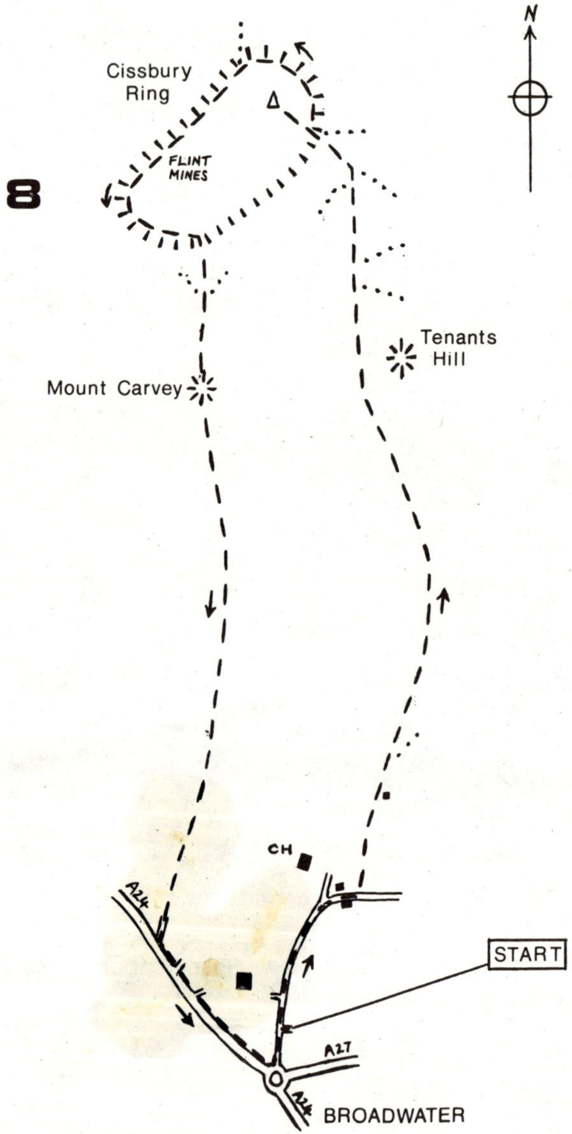
8
Cissbury Ring
FLINT MINES
N
Tenants Hill
Mount Carvey
CH
A24
START
A27
A24
BROADWATER

Walk 8
CISSBURY RING

Broadwater — Tenants Hill — Cissbury Ring — Mount Carvey — Broadwater

Distance 5 mls **Climbing** 450 ft **Highest point** 602 ft

Starting point The parking area at the entrance to the recreation ground in Hill Barn Lane, about 100 yards north of the A24/A27 roundabout at Broadwater (map reference TQ 142051).

The downs are rich in prehistoric hillforts, constructed in an age when all human settlements were on the summits of hills, and needed protection from the dangers of the Wealden forest and foreign invaders. One of the largest of these is Cissbury Ring, now a National Trust property. Originally a primitive factory where flints were mined and shaped, it was fortified in the Iron Age by a double rampart with a ditch between, enclosing an area of some 60 acres. Cissbury is well worth a visit to see not only these impressive earthworks but also the extensive view over unspoiled downland. The walk is an easy one on gentle gradients and is well provided with public seats.

Walk northward up Hill Barn Lane and follow it when it curves R to pass the flint Waterworks Cottages. About 100 yards further on turn L, to head north once more on a tree-lined bridleway. Emerging from the trees near a flint barn R, go straight on beyond a wooden gate along a track which will bring you into open country, with the Hill Barn golf course in the valley L. Beyond it is Mount Carvey and to your R the long hump of Tenants Hill.

After 1½ miles of steady climbing the valley L ends abruptly, and you will see the high inner rampart of Cissbury Ring just a few yards ahead. Go through the gate at the boundary of the National Trust property, pass through the gap in the embankment and make for the trig point at the summit (602 feet).

Chanctonbury Ring's tree clump is conspicuous in the north, while to its R is the long, high ridge carrying the South Downs Way. Due east are tree-capped Coombe Hill and Lancing Clump, with the bare dome of Steep Down between. Southward lies the coastal plain beyond Brighton in the east and Littlehampton in the west, while inland to the west stand Blackpatch, Kithurst and Barns Farm Hills.

For the exhilarating walk along the top of the rampart, return to the entrance gap, go up the steps L and set off anti-clockwise. You will notice the especially fine view of Findon in the valley on the west side, and if at this point you venture towards the centre of the Ring for a few yards you will discover the almost unearthly landscape left by the Neolithic flint miners.

Walk right round to the south side of the rampart, and leave the hillfort by a broad track going due south through a kissing gate and beside a small wood L. Now go straight on along the barely noticeable summit of Mount Carvey: Findon Valley is the modern development on your R. Soon the golf course reappears L and later you are walking through the middle of it as you head south towards Worthing. About 1½ miles from Cissbury you will arrive on the Worthing-London trunk road. Turn L along the roadside footpath, and when you reach the big roundabout at Broadwater, go L up Hill Barn Lane to regain your starting point.

Walk 9

BRAMBER CASTLE

Sompting — Lychpole Farm — Sopers Bottom — Maudlin Farm — Bramber Castle — Bramber — Annington — Annington Hill — Sompting

Distance 11½ mls **Climbing** 1100 ft **Highest point** 458 ft

Starting point The grass car park of Church Lane, Sompting, just south of the churchyard (map reference TQ 162056), by kind permission of the Vicar.

A truly exhilarating walk, right across the downland range from south to north and back again, incorporating a visit to the interest-packed little village of Bramber.

From the car park find the east-west path behind the hedge along its southern boundary. Walk along this for about 200 yards, turn R at a crosspaths and pass the church R as you steadily climb a low down called The Nore. At the top, look back for a view which embraces Shoreham Airport, Lancing, Sompting, Worthing and the isolated, tree-crowned Highdown Hill.

Now follow the same path westward, turn R at the end of the field and in another 200 yards go through a small gate. A few yards further on your path is joined by a bridleway from the L. Bear R to pass the large, flint Coombe Barn R. Beyond it, head uphill in a north-easterly direction — towards the prominent Steep Down — but soon descend northward into a valley containing farm buildings. Go through a large gate and bear R to make for the farm, called Beggars Bush. After passing a barn L, turn L along a concrete bridleway which in less than ½ mile leads into Lychpole Farm, a delightful collection of flint buildings, including barns, sheds and farmhouse.

Follow the same track (no longer concreted) as it winds through the farm and then turns R, offering a view L of the scrub-clad ridge which culminates in the hillfort of Cissbury

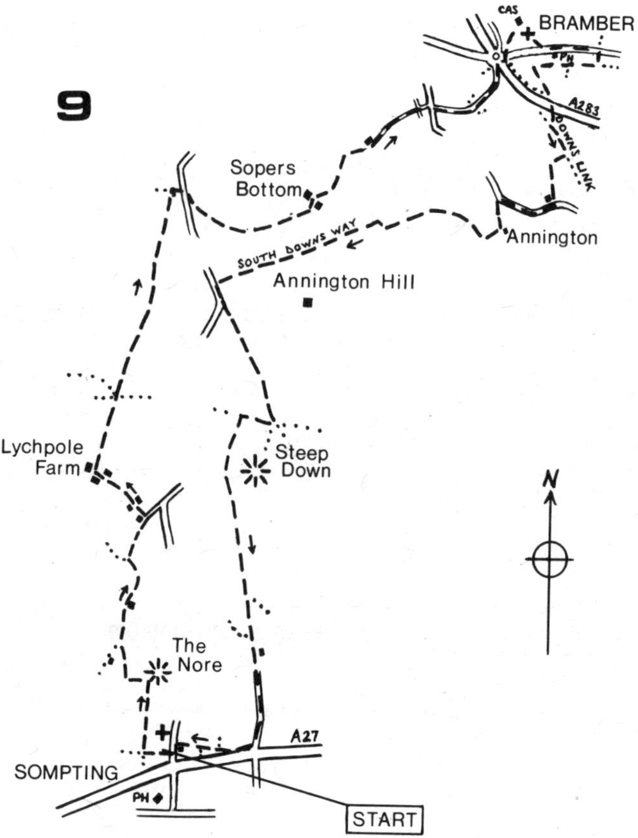
9
CAS
BRAMBER
PH
A283
DOWNS LINK
Sopers
Bottom
SOUTH DOWNS WAY
Annington
Annington Hill
Lychpole
Farm
Steep
Down
N
The
Nore
A27
SOMPTING
PH
START

Ring. At the next crosspaths go straight on northward for about 1 mile, along a steadily rising track. When you meet a concrete track turn R, and in 50 yards cross the high bostal road to take another concrete bridleway opposite, leading down to a broad valley often used for hang-gliding. In just over a mile pass the farm buildings of Sopers Bottom and continue along the same lane as it opens up a view R to Truleigh Hill and the sprawling village of Upper Beeding. After passing Upper Maudlin Farm and some pleasing modern houses, you will emerge on the Steyning-Coombes road. Walk R for a few yards and then turn L into Maudlin Lane, which in ½ mile will bring you to the roundabout just below Bramber Castle.

Bramber has much to interest the sightseer. Its dominant feature is the ruin of a Norman castle, a National Trust property to which there is free admission and ample space for picnics. Just below, on the same hillock, is the Norman church of St Nicholas, a remnant of the original cruciform building which once served as the castle's chapel. The village contains also a museum, gift shops, pubs, cafes and restaurants.

Walk east along the village street, and just after passing the half-timbered St Mary's, take a footpath R, cross a footbridge, and follow the signposted right of way around the southern boundary of a caravan site. In about 200 yards turn L and head south across a field to the main Shoreham-Steyning road. Cross it, bear R and 100 yards farther on turn L to walk along the line of the former Horsham railway track, now part of the 30-mile Downs Link.

After just over ¼ mile leave the Downs Link by a footpath R which goes west, then south around the edge of a field, to emerge on the Coombes road at the tiny hamlet of Annington. Now turn R, and walk up the lane past a farm and some large residences. Just after the last house R, turn L at the top of the road and take the leafy track signposted 'South Downs Way'. At the entrance to Tinpots Cottage turn R and follow all South Downs Way signs as the route ascends Annington Hill, revealing views L of the Adur, meandering into Shoreham past the conspicuous gothic chapel of Lancing College, and R to Steyning, Bramber, Beeding and the floodplains of the Adur.

The Way is steep at first, but becomes almost level along the broad summit of Annington Hill. Eventually it brings you once more on to the bostal road. Turn L along the roadside path for 80 yards, and then bear L to walk south on a track towards the domed shape of Steep Down. At a crosspaths beside a tall transmission tower turn R, and in another 100 yards take a L turn. Continue along this southward track for 1½ miles, until it arrives at the Brighton-Worthing trunk road.

Now go R along the tarmac path, and in 100 yards find a path R leading through young trees to an iron kissing gate. Pass through this, and walk along the northern edge of a field until you emerge once more in Church Lane, just south of Sompting church.

The famous parish church of St Mary the Virgin is well worth a visit. Its unusual but elegant tower, commonly called a 'Rhenish Helm', is of a type found in the Rhine valley but unique in Britain. The interior is equally interesting, with numerous traces of Saxon sculpture and Norman decoration.

Bramber Castle

Walk 10

CHANCTONBURY AND THE SOUTH DOWNS WAY

Steyning — Wiston — Washington — Chanctonbury Ring — Steyning Round Hill — Steyning

Distance 10 mls **Climbing** 900 ft **Highest point** 783 ft

Starting point The large car park immediately south of Steyning parish church (map reference TQ 179113).

The route goes outward along the foot of the downs below Chanctonbury Ring and returns over its summit, using a 3½ mile length of the lofty South Downs Way.

Turn L opposite the church, go R down the road just past the lychgate and in 50 yards L again into Tanyard Lane. Follow this for ¼ mile to its junction with Steyning High Street and turn R. In another 200 yards, when the main thoroughfare bends R, go straight on into Mouse Lane. This is a narrow, leafy lane which at most times of the year has a babbling stream on its R side for the first ¼ mile.

Walk along Mouse Lane for nearly 1 mile until you are in sight of the entrance gateway to Wilton Park. About 20 yards short of it find a footpath L, which in 50 yards veers R and soon crosses both a stream and a stile into a field. Your path runs along the R side of this field with a line of trees R and Chanctonbury's familiar group of beeches prominent on the hill ahead. At the far end of the field, as Wiston's grey Elizabethan Manor house appears R, turn L along a lane and pass under a quaint footbridge. Keep straight on when the surface deteriorates and later pass through a farm with a granary R, standing on mushroom staddle stones.

A few yards farther on, turn R on another surfaced lane, but almost at once go L to resume your westward route along a bridleway between hedges. In ¼ mile this track enters the woods cloaking the lower slopes of Chanctonbury and rises a

10

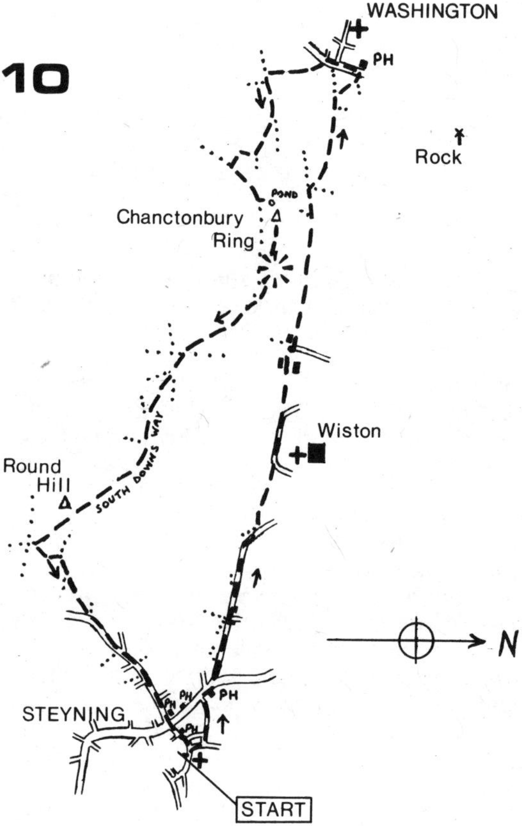
WASHINGTON
PH
Rock
POND
Chanctonbury
Ring
Wiston
Round
Hill
SOUTH DOWNS WAY
N
PH
PH
PH
PH
STEYNING
START

little, still keeping close to the woods' edge. In a further ¼ mile go through a metal gate, pass a barn R, and climb a short way into the woods L. Then bear R to begin the gentle descent through the woods by way of a further iron gate. When eventually you leave the wood, take a diagonal path north-west across 2 fields, noting the black, sweepless smock mill R, beside the sand quarries. Rock mill, built early in the 19th century, was converted into a private residence in 1919 and was for some years the home of composer John Ireland.

After ¼ mile bear L by a hedge, and walk west along the northern edge of a field, with Barns Farm Hill on the skyline ahead. Just before reaching the western end of the field cross a stile to enter a small, sloping meadow R. Descend across it, pass over a wooden footbridge and emerge by way of a kissing gate opposite the Frankland Arms at Washington.

Now go south along the old Worthing road for 300 yards and then L over a stile opposite Stocks Mead. Follow a footpath south-easterly across a field and cross another stile into the woods. Now the path climbs steeply for a short distance through the trees, but evens out as it passes a chalk quarry R. At the quarry entrance join a broader track which in 200 yards meets the South Downs Way at right angles. Turn L here, and make the long ascent of the downs along the Washington bostal path, with ever-widening views to west and south.

After nearly a mile of continuous climbing turn L where the Way is joined by the bridleway R from Findon. Chanctonbury Ring now beckons, but before attaining its summit be sure to visit the dewpond and trig point L. They are described in Walk 7.

Leave the Ring by its east side and continue along the South Downs Way south-easterly along almost level ground on the 600 foot contour for nearly 2 miles. As you pass the trig point R atop Steyning Round Hill (619 feet), a superb view unfolds over Steyning, Bramber and Upper Beeding, with their green backcloth formed by the downland range around Truleigh Hill. Just over 200 yards farther on, before reaching a metal gate across the path, leave the South Downs Way to find a path L in front of some scrub growth and then beside a fence R. In 100 yards this crosses the fence line and descends on the other side.

At a T-junction of paths above a deep coombe go R and walk down the southern arm of the Horseshoe. In ¼ mile fork L and drop steeply down the hillside to join Newham Lane, which you must follow all the way into Steyning. Cross the High Street into Church Street, and pass the ancient Grammar School buildings to regain your starting point in the car park.

Steyning is well worth exploring. The sturdy Norman church of St Andrew is built on the site of an 8th century church founded by a Sussex saint called Cuthman. The exterior is remarkable for the chequered pattern on the tower, while inside are some splendid ornamental arches and mouldings. The little town is full of delightful vernacular buildings of particularly the 15th and 19th centuries, including the grammar school, a prison and a workhouse. There is a museum, 4 pubs and a rich assortment of restaurants.

Steyning

Walk 11

ADUR MEADOWS AND WOODS MILL

Steyning — Kings Barn Bridge — Newhall Farm — Woods Mill/Small Dole — Newhall Farm — Stretham Bridge — Wyckham Farm — Kings Barn Farm — Steyning

Distance 9 mls **Climbing** 150 ft **Highest point** 80 ft

Starting point The large car park immediately south of Steyning parish church (map reference TQ 179113).

Not really a downland walk, but it does offer extensive and unforgettable views of the downs from the north. There is a pleasant stretch along the east bank of the Adur, a visit to the natural history centre at Woods Mill and a return along part of the Downs Link, a recently opened long distance bridleway which makes good use of the track of the Shoreham-Horsham railway, closed in 1966.

Cross the wooden footbridge east of the car park and turn R along a tarmac path across the green. Go L in front of a flint wall, then cross a road and walk up Holland Road ahead. At a T-junction go straight on through a twitten between close-boarded fences which leads to a footbridge over the Shoreham road (here in a cutting of the disused railway track). Resume the path beside Down House R, and pass the Castlefield Stores. After crossing another road go down Castle Way and then down a footpath opposite which passes between bungalows. Now turn L to walk along a path beside a brook. Go over a stile and continue by the brook for ¼ mile until you cross a small footbridge R; then walk east across the meadows to iron Kings Barn Bridge over the Adur. Ahead Truleigh Hill looms behind the church and rectory of Upper Beeding, while on your R the square tower of Bramber church is backed by Annington Hill.

Cross the river and go L along the eastern bank for about 1½ miles. As it sweeps eastward, note the line of downs from Wolstonbury in the far east, through Newtimber, Dyke,

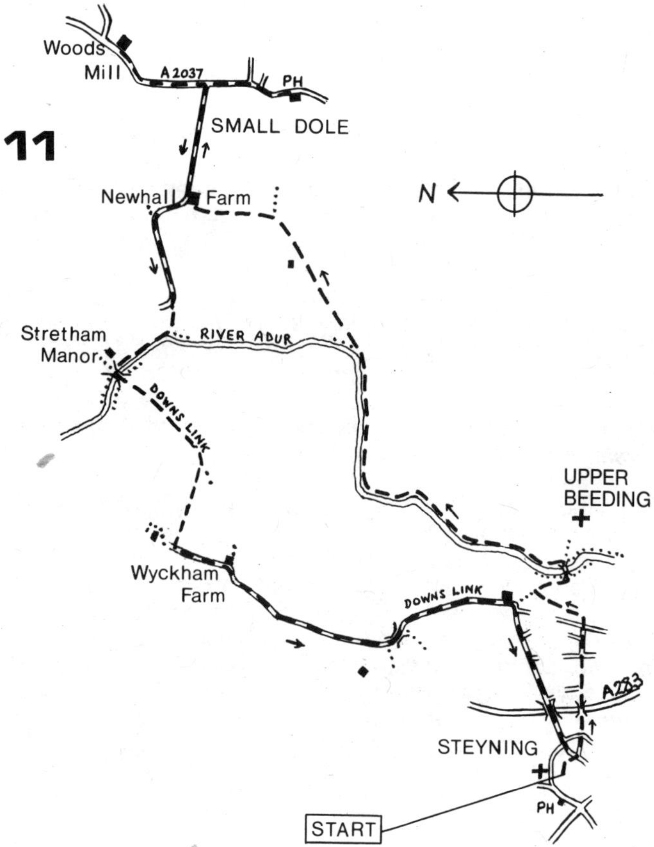

11
Woods Mill
A2037
PH
SMALL DOLE
N
Newhall Farm
Stretham Manor
RIVER ADUR
DOWNS LINK
UPPER BEEDING
Wyckham Farm
DOWNS LINK
A283
STEYNING
PH
START

Perching, Edburton and Truleigh Hills, with Tottington Mount nearest. At a sharp L bend in the river near a belt of trees, cross another stile to leave the riverbank and walk north-east along the R side of a raised field for about 200 yards. Then follow the path as it veers L, and soon cross a rough road leading to a refuse tip. Continue in the same direction towards a low, flint barn. Pass south of this and enter the corner of Horton Wood. Follow the footpath signs for 100 yards and then leave the wood to head north across a large field to Newhall Farm on the ridge ahead.

After crossing a plank bridge walk up a narrow path and enter the farm. Now turn R, follow the lane through the farm and head east along Newhall Lane. On arriving on the main road to Henfield you have a choice. The Fox and Hounds at Small Dole is ½ mile to the R, while the same distance to the L is Woods Mill.

The headquarters of the Sussex Trust for Nature Conservation, the 17th century watermill and buildings are now converted into a fascinating nature centre, complete with guided nature trail around its extensive lakeside and woodland grounds. The centre is open from Easter to the end of September (other than on Mondays and Fridays), afternoons only; on Sundays and bank holidays, however, it opens at 11 am. There is a charge for admission.

Return along Newhall Lane. On reaching the bungalow at its end turn R along a lane which curves L to pass an isolated red-brick house. Now you are on a section of Roman road, which ran across the Sussex Weald to ford the Adur at Stretham. Follow this in the direction of Chanctonbury until a R bend. Then take a footpath L and continue towards Chanctonbury to rejoin the riverbank. Here go R, and cross the Adur by an iron bridge which once carried the railway from Shoreham to Horsham. To your R is the medieval, tile-hung Stretham Manor.

Once on the bridge, go straight on along the Downs Link bridleway, which uses the old railway track here for the next ½ mile. At a point where a gate on either side signifies a former crossing of the line, leave the track to continue along the Downs Link, which now proceeds uphill towards Wyckham Manor in the west. Emerging on a rough track just south of a low barn, turn L, and proceed along a winding lane for the next 1½ miles, noting once again fine views of the downs to east and west.

At Kings Barn Farm on the outskirts of Steyning go R along Kings Barn Lane and in less than ½ mile cross a road bridge over the main road, near the site of Steyning station. Soon the main lane bears R, but you must go straight on along Jarvis Lane. In another 200 yards turn R opposite Holland Road and walk through a twitten to regain your starting point in the car park.

Woods Mill

Walk 12

BEEDING HILL AND BOTOLPHS

Bramber — Upper Beeding — Windmill Hill — Golding Barn — Beeding Hill — Botolphs — Bramber

Distance 6 mls **Climbing** 470 ft **Highest point** 375 ft

Starting point The car park in Bramber High Street (map reference TQ 187107), opposite the House of Pipes museum.

An easy and delightful short walk, visiting 2 ancient churches and 2 of the best viewpoints in the Adur valley.

Leaving the car park turn L along Bramber Street and pass St Mary's, a large, timber-framed house erected in the 15th century for the monks of the Priory at Beeding, the wardens of the old Bramber bridge. Just before the road crosses the bridge, go down some steps L on to the bank of the Adur. Walk north along the riverbank path, and soon notice views L to Steyning Round Hill and Chanctonbury, and R to Truleigh and Beeding Hills.

After ½ mile cross the river by an iron footbridge, turn R and walk back along the eastern bank as far as the next bend. Now turn L to cross a ditch by a little wooden footbridge, and ascend a flight of steps to the entrance to Upper Beeding church.

It is likely that a church existed here before the Norman Conquest, but this was rebuilt in 1070, and 10 years later assumed a new importance when it became a priory church, adjacent to the Benedictine priory of Sele. The oldest surviving parts of the present building, dedicated to St Peter, date from the 11th century.

Walk on down the lane eastward, and then straight on along Deacons Way. At a T-junction turn R into Pound Lane, and after passing the shops of Hyde Square take the next turning L. In another 200 yards go L along a made-up footpath and at its end cross the road to find another path on the opposite side. This climbs to reach a further road, where you

12

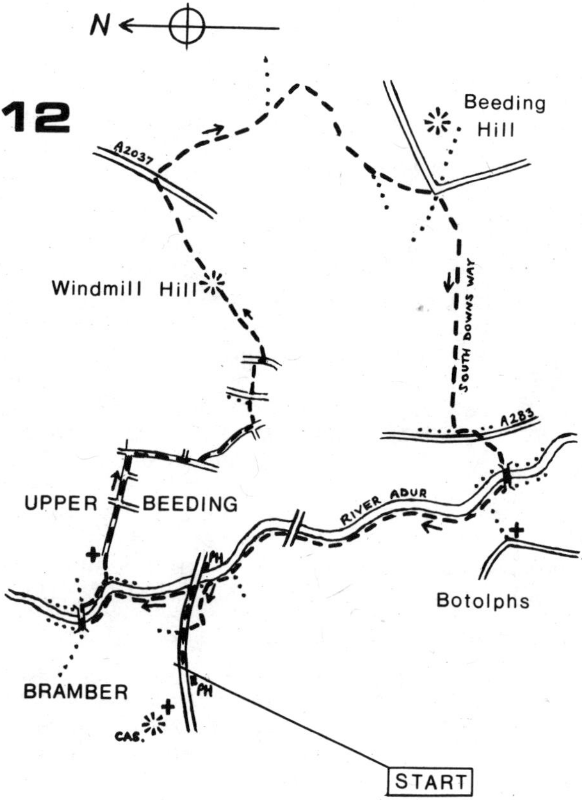

N
Beeding Hill
A2037
Windmill Hill
SOUTH DOWNS WAY
A283
RIVER ADUR
UPPER BEEDING
PH
Botolphs
BRAMBER
PH
CAS.
START

must turn R for 100 yards and then go L to leave the built-up area by a footpath which ascends Windmill Hill (196 feet).

The windmill has long since vanished, but this little hill is a good viewpoint because of its isolation from the main block of downs. Notice especially the panorama of green hills lining the western side of the valley — Lancing Clump (with the College chapel and Coombes hamlet below), Coombe Hill (and Botolphs at its foot), Steep Down, Annington Hill, Steyning Round Hill and Chanctonbury, with Steyning and Bramber villages spread out beneath. To the north there is a good view over the Weald, irrigated by the tributary brooks of the meandering Adur.

Continue over the hill to the Henfield road, go L in front of the petrol station, cross the road at Golding Barn and walk up the concrete bridleway opposite. After passing a farm, continue the climb as the bridle path passes through trees, and at a clearing bear R to take the lower of 2 paths. This is a particularly pleasing section, which passes through the deep coombe below Tottington Mount, whose slopes rise L with mountain-like steepness, and ascends steadily to arrive eventually by the 6-armed fingerpost just below the summit of Beeding Hill at 375 feet.

The view westward is similar to that from Windmill Hill, but now you can see the Channel beyond Lancing College, the hillfort at Cissbury (on the horizon behind Botolphs) and the village of Upper Beeding, spread out at your feet.

Now take the airy path signposted 'South Downs Way', along the ridge on the north side of Anchor Bottom, in the direction of Botolphs. The path drops down to the Shoreham-Steyning road, where you must turn L along the tarmac path for about 80 yards and then cross the road to a footbridge over the Adur. Pass over this, and turn R to continue along the western riverbank. If you have time, leave it soon afterwards to cross the line of the old Shoreham-Horsham railway for a visit to Botolphs church.

Dedicated to the 7th century English saint Botolph, the church has Saxon work in the nave and chancel walls, and a Saxon chancel arch. It has also a rare Jacobean carved pulpit, complete with sounding board. Botolphs is now no more than a lonely, picturesque hamlet, but once it was a prosperous settlement on the banks of a river where large ships sailed up to Bramber Castle and Sele Priory.

Resume the riverbank path, and about a mile from the South Downs Way footbridge take a footpath L, alongside a hedge (just before arriving back at Bramber road bridge). Walk for about 200 yards parallel with the road, which is only a few yards away. Then turn R to pass over a small footbridge into Bramber Street, where a L turn will bring you back to the cafes, shops and car park at Bramber.

Upper Beeding

Walk 13

STEEP DOWN AND ANNINGTON HILL

North Lancing — Lancing Clump — Steep Down — Annington Hill — Coombes — Cow Bottom — Lancing Hill — North Lancing

Distance 6½ mls **Climbing** 650 ft **Highest point** 489 ft

Starting point The rough parking area just beyond the northern end of Mill Road, North Lancing (map reference TQ 183063). This is reached by a flinty track which goes past a reservoir L on to the open downs.

An airy walk over the hills behind Lancing, including the stiff climb of Steep Down to enjoy its panoramic view, a steady 1½ mile descent along the South Downs Way and a visit to the secluded hamlet of Coombes.

Set off northward along the flint bridleway past a disused chalk pit and some riding stables R, and continue the ascent to pass Lancing Clump L, a distinctive line of well-established beeches. Just over the crest of the hill, notice the prominent dome of Steep Down ahead, with Cissbury and Chanctonbury in attendance behind it on either side. Pursue the same track as it goes north-west, until just before it begins to wind around the north side of the hill. At the end of the field L, you must turn L at a signpost and in 20 yards find R the straight and obvious path which will lead you to the trig point on the summit, at 489 feet.

The view from the top of Steep Down is extensive. On a clear day the coastline may be traced from Beachy Head in the east to Littlehampton in the west, and acres of rolling downland are revealed on all sides. In the west, Highdown is the diminutive, tree-crowned hill nearest the sea, while north of it stretches the long, high ridge terminating in the Iron Age hillfort of Cissbury Ring. North-west stand Chanctonbury's beeches, and R of them is Steyning Round Hill; north-east is Coombe Hill — also tree-topped — with the village of Upper

13

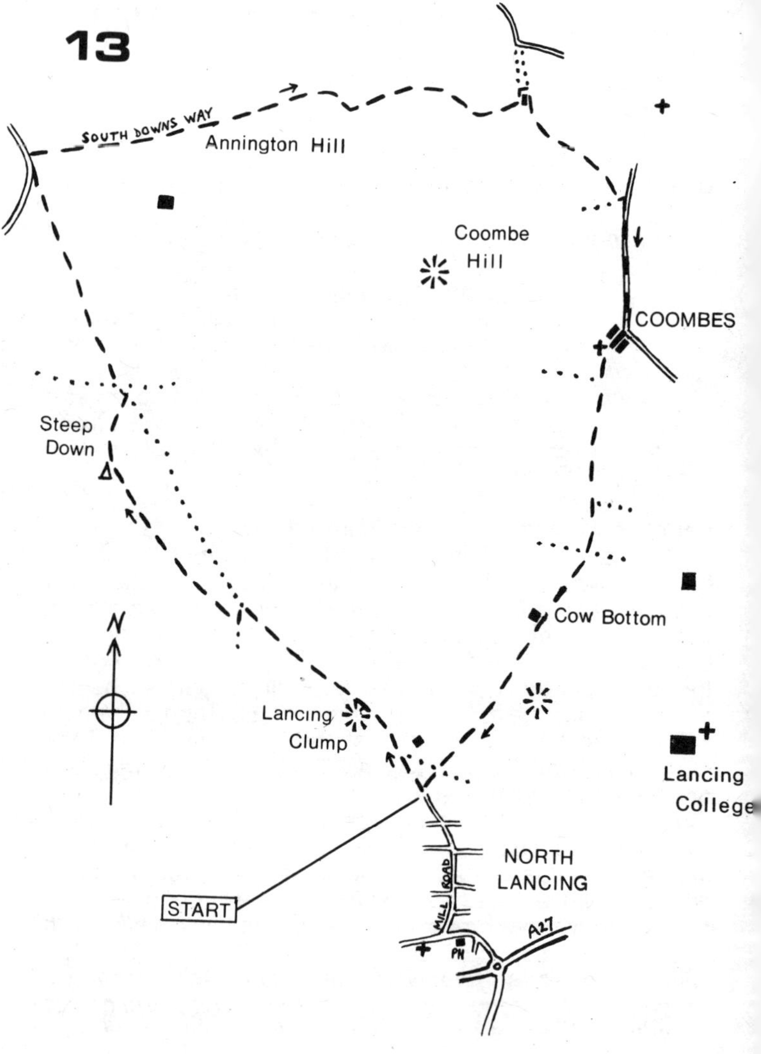
SOUTH DOWNS WAY
Annington Hill
Coombe
Hill
COOMBES
Steep
Down
Cow Bottom
Lancing
Clump
Lancing
College
NORTH
LANCING
MILL ROAD
START
PH
A27
N

Beeding and the bulky mass of Truleigh Hill beyond. Lancing Clump is south-east, in front of Shoreham and the silvery Adur.

Now follow the same path as it descends north to a tall transmission tower. Beside it, go through a gate L and then due north towards the top of a hill surmounted by some prominent barns. In ½ mile you will join the road from Sompting to Steyning, which fortunately has a grass path on its R side. After only a few yards, take the path R, signposted 'South Downs Way', and stay on it as it gradually descends in the direction of Beeding, with a fence L, separating you from the deep Maudlin valley. When the Way bears R, follow it uphill to a metal gate L, and after passing through this continue the eastward descent towards distant Truleigh Hill and later the incongruous cement works.

On reaching a shed near Tinpots Cottage, follow your path L for about 20 yards, and then find a bridleway through the trees R. After going through a wooden gate, turn R to head south, with the Adur valley on your L. When this path ends at an iron gate, pass through it and in 20 yards by way of a wooden gate enter a small wood. Go uphill out of it, turn L along a bridleway for a few yards, and emerge on a road opposite the cement works. Now turn R and walk along the roadside for a bit less than ½ mile until arriving at a telephone kiosk by the lane to Coombes. Go R here, walk the length of the tiny street, and by way of 2 squeezer stiles enter the church.

Coombes church, unusual in not being dedicated to a saint or saints, is a small, unspoiled downland church with a Norman nave and a chancel only century younger. Within are 12th century wall paintings, discovered in 1949 and beautifully restored.

Now walk south through the churchyard and leave it by another squeezer stile into a wood. Follow the path uphill until it emerges on open down, and proceed south over the brow of the hill to join a path with a wire fence R. As Lancing College comes into view L, cross a stile and continue south with the same fence L. Avoid the temptation to go down a broad track L, but go straight on with a line of trees L and cross another track leading from Valley Barn to Applesham Farm in the valley. After descending to the remote valley called Cow Bottom, with its flint enclosure, go through a small gate and ascend Lancing Hill by a steep path between fences.

At the top of the climb, cross a stile L and continue across the broad ridge between Lancing Hill and Lancing Clump. Note the fine view north-west to Steep Down, Chanctonbury and Coombe Hill. Go straight across the large field which straddles the ridge, and make for a stile leading to a field beside the riding stables. On the opposite side of this field cross a further stile to emerge on the path from Hoe Court, near the chalk pit which you passed at the start of the walk. This is the site of a former windmill, and is close to your starting point, R.

Coombes

Walk 14
COOMBES

Sussex Pad — Hoe Court — Lancing Clump — Coombe Hill — Coombes — Cuckoo's Corner — Sussex Pad

Distance 7 mls **Climbing** 510 ft **Highest point** 358 ft

Starting point The lane beside Pad farmhouse, just north of the Sussex Pad hotel, North Lancing (map reference TQ 200061).

An easy walk on well-defined paths north of Lancing and along the bank of the Adur.

Walk up the lane behind Pad Farm, noting the prominent chapel of Lancing College across the field R. In 200 yards fork L to take a bridleway climbing steadily between bushes and on to open downland for a close view of the College buildings.

Lancing College was founded in 1848 by Nathaniel Woodard, then parish curate in Shoreham. It was the first of 15 schools founded by Woodard before his death in 1891, his aim being 'the union of classes by a common system of education'. Buildings have been added at regular intervals since the pupils first moved on to this site in 1858, the lofty Gothic chapel having taken over 100 years to complete.

Continue along the bridleway, passing Hoe Court cottages R, some larger residences L and a riding stables R before arriving on the crest of a hill surmounted by the trees known as Lancing Clump. Look back to observe the eastern view of the coastline stretching away to Seaford Head and Beachy Head, and of the downland range, dominated by Truleigh Hill. As you pass over the crest of the hill you will see Cissbury Ring, Steep Down and Chanctonbury Ring across the way ahead.

Now keep going north-west, along the terraced path which skirts the north side of Steep Down. Eventually this descends to a meeting of paths near a tall pylon. Here, go through a gate R to take a bridleway which heads east along the top of a high ridge towards tree-topped Coombe Hill. Pass the trees L and

14

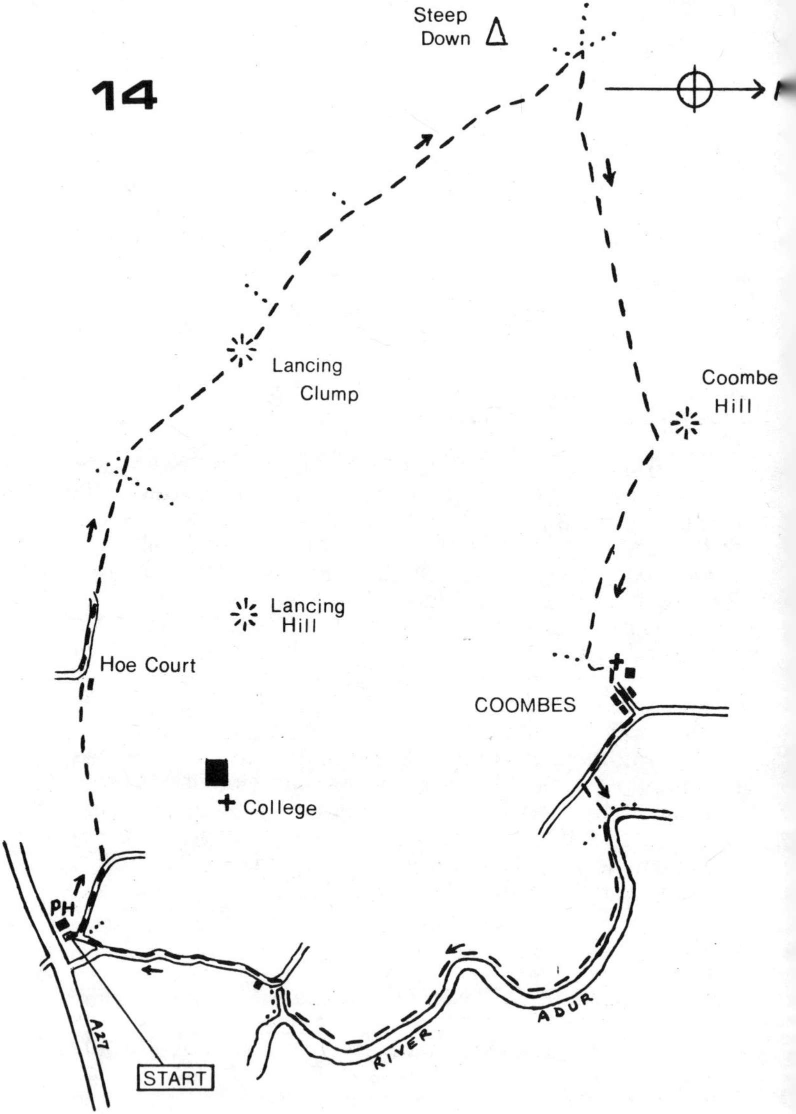
Steep Down
Lancing Clump
Coombe Hill
Lancing Hill
Hoe Court
COOMBES
College
PH
A27
START
RIVER
ADUR

then begin to descend gently, first towards the cement works and then in the direction of Shoreham and the Adur. In the coombe (valley) ahead lies the sleepy hamlet of Coombes — just a tiny church, a farm and a few cottages.

Keeping a fence close R, you will come at length to a gate just above a wood, L. Pass through it, and then descend by a sometimes slippery path through the wood to emerge in Coombes churchyard, which you enter by a squeezer stile. The church is described in Walk 13. Leave the churchyard by a tapsell gate, descend the L side of a field, with the Old Rectory on its far side, and pass through another squeezer into the lane leading to the Steyning road.

Turn R on reaching the road, but in about 300 yards find a footpath L which heads in the direction of the cement works and brings you on to the bank of the river Adur. Once there, go R along the riverbank as it follows one of the Adur's larger meanders for about 1½ miles. On arriving at the creek at Cuckoo's Corner, rejoin the road and walk south until you regain your start at the Sussex Pad.

Lancing College

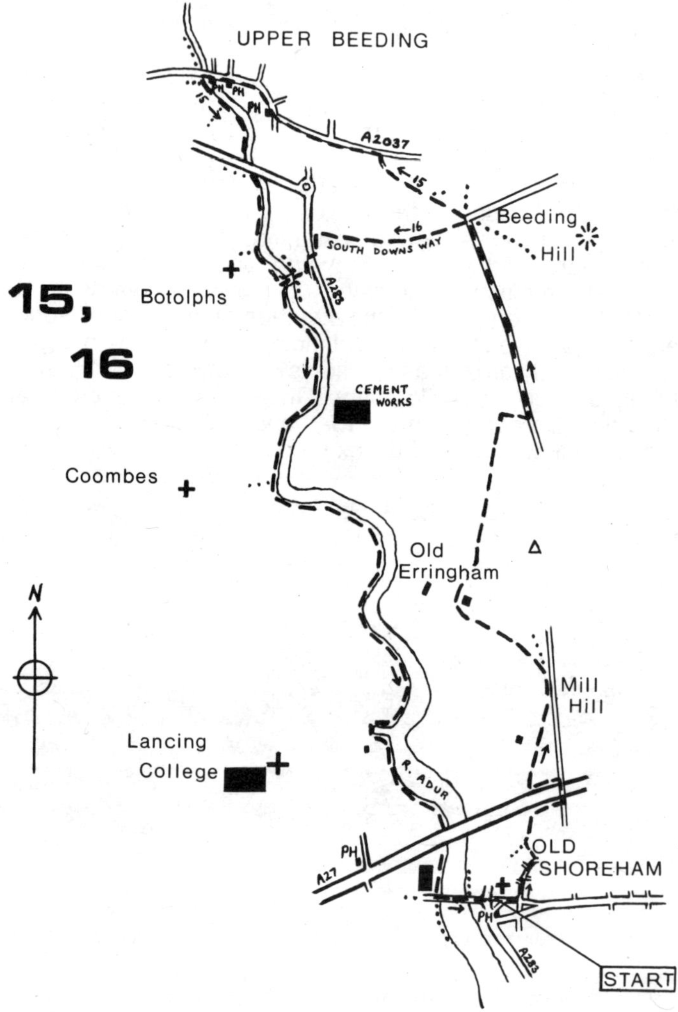
UPPER BEEDING
PH
PH
PH
15
A2037
15
Beeding
Hill
16
SOUTH DOWNS WAY
A283
15,
16
Botolphs
CEMENT
WORKS
Coombes
Old
Erringham
N
Mill
Hill
Lancing
College
R. ADUR
PH
A27
OLD
SHOREHAM
PH
A283
START

Walk 15

ADUR VALLEY TO BEEDING

Old Shoreham — Mill Hill — Old Erringham — Beeding Hill — Upper Beeding — Botolphs — Cuckoo's Corner — Old Shoreham

Distance 9½ mls **Climbing** 410 ft **Highest point** 406 ft

Starting point The blocked-up lane on the south side of Old Shoreham churchyard (map reference TQ 208060).

An easy stroll on mainly firm paths and gentle gradients, except for one steep descent. A feature of the walk is the opportunity to study at close range the flora and fauna of both downland and riverside. A shorter alternative is at Walk 16.

Walk east along St Nicolas Lane and turn L up The Street of Old Shoreham village, passing an attractive mixture of modern homes and ancient cottages, some with thatched roofs. In ¼ mile at a sharp R bend take a footpath L, opposite the high flint walls of Adur House. This brings you at once on to the downs above the A27 flyover, opened in 1970. Follow the path west at first, then north, along the perimeter of a field overlooking the broad river valley.

On reaching the cutting made to accommodate the Shoreham bypass follow the diverted path R, observing a fine view south to the two Shorehams, dominated by their Norman church towers, and south-west to the airport, one of the early centres of aviation in Britain. Cross the bypass by a graceful concrete road bridge, and immediately afterwards go L to resume the path along the edge of the escarpment. Arriving at a green space well provided with seats, pause to take in the extensive and beautiful view to the west.

The chapel of Lancing College is prominent; behind it stands Lancing Clump, while to its R the skyline embraces the summits of Steep Down, Steyning Round Hill and Chanctonbury Ring. Below them are tree-crowned Coombe Hill and the tiny hamlets of Applesham and Coombes.

Now resume your walk northward towards Mill Hill. About 100 yards before the green hump of a downland reservoir fork L to descend by a path running along the foot of the famous 'butterfly bank'. In appropriate months of the year this is an excellent spot to observe typical flora and fauna of the Sussex downs, particularly the Chalk Hill and Adonis Blue butterflies and their colourful foodplant, the Horseshoe Vetch. Continue along the path into a patch of hawthorn bushes, and beyond them cross a stile to proceed towards Old Erringham Farm.

Enter the farm by a stile beside a large gate, bear R around the west side of some flint barns, pass through a second gate and head towards a third, at the northern end of the field. Erringham was mentioned in Domesday Book, and although now but a farm it still possesses a Norman chapel, used as a barn, just R of the three modern tile-hung houses to the west. Cross a stile beside the third gate and set off northward along a gently rising path. In about ½ mile this ends abruptly, and you must turn R to emerge in a further 200 yards on the high lane from Shoreham. Turn L, and walk beside the lane, climbing steadily to the highest point of the walk, where the lane is crossed by a line of transmission wires. A little way further on, you will arrive at the viewpoint just below the top of Beeding Hill, described in Walk 12.

WALKS 15 AND 16 DIVERGE HERE.

Now walk down the rough track leading north-west in the direction of Chanctonbury and Steyning. This drops steeply between the hawthorn hedgerows to emerge on the Beeding — Henfield road. At the road junction turn L along the tarmac path, and in ¼ mile arrive at the Rising Sun public house. Go R and follow the main street through Upper Beeding, with its interesting half-timbered and knapped-flint cottages. If you have time, go along the lane R opposite the Kings Head, to visit St Peter's church, detailed in Walk 12. Return to the village street and cross the bridge over the Adur. Immediately afterwards take the riverbank path L, and walk beside the meandering Adur all the way back to Old Shoreham. First you will pass under a concrete bridge and soon afterwards come close to the ancient church of St Botolph, which also is described in Walk 12. Next you pass the modern footbridge built to take the South Downs Way across the river.

WALKS 15 AND 16 REUNITE HERE.

Walk on past the huge cement works, and later observe Coombes R and Old Erringham L, before leaving the riverbank momentarily at the narrow creek known as Cuckoo's Corner. Back beside the Adur, pass under the low, functional, box-girder bridge carrying the Brighton-Worthing trunk road, and then cross the river by the quaint timber-trestle bridge which it replaced. Built in 1781, Old Shoreham Bridge bore the heavy trunk road traffic until 1970, but is now a footbridge, well restored by the County Council in 1985. It will return you to your starting point near St Nicolas's church.

Old Shoreham Bridge

Old Shoreham

Walk 16

ADUR VALLEY TO BOTOLPHS

Old Shoreham — Mill Hill — Old Erringham — Beeding Hill — Botolphs Bridge — Cuckoo's Corner — Old Shoreham

Distance 7½ mls **Climbing** 410 ft **Highest point** 406 ft

Starting point The blocked-up lane on the south side of Old Shoreham churchyard (map reference TQ 208060).

A slightly shorter version of Walk 15.

Follow Walk 15 as far as the viewpoint near the top of Beeding Hill. Then take the path L, signposted 'South Downs Way', which proceeds westward along the northern lip of Anchor Bottom. As the descent becomes more pronounced, notice the Saxon church of St Botolph ahead, just beyond the river. Arriving at the Shoreham — Petworth road, turn L along the tarmac path, and in 80 yards cross the road to a lane leading to the resumption of the South Downs Way, which here crosses the Adur by a metal bridge opened in 1974. The remainder of your route is described under Walk 15.

17

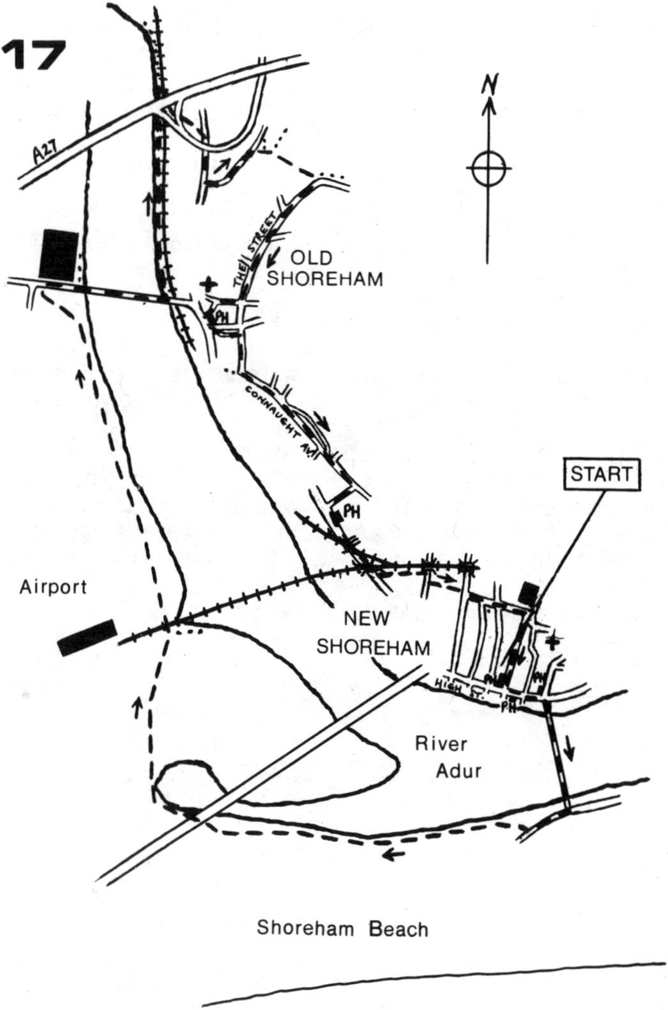
A27
N
OLD
SHOREHAM
THE STREET
PH
CONNAUGHT AV.
PH
START
Airport
NEW
SHOREHAM
HIGH ST.
PH
PH
PH
River
Adur
Shoreham Beach

Walk 17

HISTORIC SHOREHAM

Shoreham High Street — footbridge — airport — Old Shoreham Bridge — Old Shoreham — Swiss Gardens — Shoreham High Street

Distance 4 mls **Climbing** 75 ft **Highest point** 75 ft

Starting point Any one of the small car parks in the side streets north of Shoreham High Street (map reference TQ 215051).

A short and easy stroll around the ancient ports of Old and New Shoreham, sandwiched between the downs and the English Channel. Allow plenty of time to pause and enjoy the many points of interest on the route.

Walk eastward along the south side of High Street and cross the Adur by the concrete footbridge, erected in 1921 to serve the growing community on the narrow peninsula of Shoreham Beach.

Between the wars there were film studios and a motley collection of bungalows here, some of them converted railway carriages and many the homes of show business celebrities. During the invasion scare of 1940 this 'Bungalow Town' was almost rased to the ground in the interests of national defence, so the development you now see south of the river is almost entirely postwar.

Turn R, and walk along the tarmac footpath for 50 yards, before taking the paved riverbank path R. This passes a long line of houseboats which form a picturesque foreground to the view of Shoreham across the river. On arriving at the road to Worthing, cross and find a footpath opposite which skirts the west side of a tidal lagoon, a haven for many gulls and waders. Continue by walking along the western edge of the Adur Recreation Ground and make for the end of the iron railway bridge. Now you are back on the riverbank as you head north, with Shoreham Airport on your L.

It was in July 1910 that a locally built plane made the first

flight from this airfield, but the present terminal dates only from 1936. For most of its life the airport has been used principally by civil light aircraft, but it has also been the home of aircraft production (Miles and Beagle) and saw active service in both world wars. Even today the Second World War leaves its mark in the shape of brick fortifications at intervals along the riverbank.

At length you will reach the approach road to timber-trestled Old Shoreham Bridge, opposite Ricardo's engineering works. Walk over the bridge, constructed originally in 1781 to carry the main south coast trunk road, a function which it performed with decreasing efficiency until 1970, when it was replaced by the flyover to the north. Its carriageway was reconstructed in 1985 to accord with its new role as a footbridge.

Turn L at the end of the bridge along the eastern riverbank, with the disused track of the Shoreham-Steyning railway R. Just after passing under the flyover note a fine view of Lancing College L and Mill Hill R. Now cross the railway track and walk south-east under the Stonehenge-type arches to emerge on the Steyning road. Walk R for about 50 yards, and after passing under the road bridge cross over and find the narrow lane to the Old Shoreham pumping station, right under the southern ridge of Mill Hill. Go through the gate, and about 20 yards further on climb the hillside R, by a path through the bushes. Pause at the top to admire the view of the broad Adur valley, and then continue along the south side of a large field, behind some modern houses. When you see the high flint walls of Adur Lodge R, descend to the village street of Old Shoreham, and walk south along it, past quaint 18th century cottages, some of them still thatched. Turn R at the old farmhouse to visit the parish church of St Nicolas.

Dedicated to the patron saint of mariners, Old Shoreham church once surveyed a broad estuary where ships sailed up to Bramber. Notice the 2 blocked Saxon doorways in the nave and the magnificent Norman architecture of the tower and transepts, particularly the mouldings and carvings of the interior tower arches.

Now turn R, pass the Red Lion Inn and cross the main road to The Amsterdam, a former vicarage of Old Shoreham. Go L in front of it, and then R into Connaught Avenue.The northern part of this road is an extension of the village street, and contains more thatched cottages, but the long, straight, southern section follows the line of the ancient field path between Old and New Shoreham. When it ends at a garden shop, turn R into Freehold Street to reach the entrance of the Swiss Gardens, L.

This is the site of the original harbour, which became silted up in the 14th century. In 1838 a local shipbuilder established here one of the finest of all Victorian pleasure grounds, complete with restaurant, games rooms, ballroom, observatory, lake and grotto. The gardens thrived until the turn of the century, when their popularity waned and large parts were sold for other uses. Now only the lake and inn remain, to attract pleasure-seekers of the 20th century.

Walk south along Old Shoreham Road, passing under 2 railway bridges before going L into a twitten running parallel with the railway. At its end cross the road and find another twitten between houses which will bring you into North Street, opposite the modern Roman Catholic church. Walk east along North Street, and opposite the Community Centre turn R into Middle Street. This will lead you to the Marlipins Museum at the junction with High Street: a unique 12th century buiding now housing many exhibits illustrating the town's maritime history and that of places visited earlier in your walk.

You are now at journey's end, but before leaving Shoreham be sure to visit the stately parish church of St Mary de Haura (of the Harbour), which dominates this little town of small-scale houses and shops. Incredibly this huge building is only a part of the original, as you can see by the ruins in the churchyard, but its late Norman architecture is impressive enough, particularly the 2-stage tower and the massive chancel pillars.

For further reading about the history of this, my home town, I recommend 'The Story of Shoreham' by Henry Cheal, 'A Walkabout Guide to Shoreham' by Michael Norman, 'Bungalow Town' by Neb Wolters, the guide to the parish churches and the RSPB leaflet, 'A Walk along the Adur'.

18

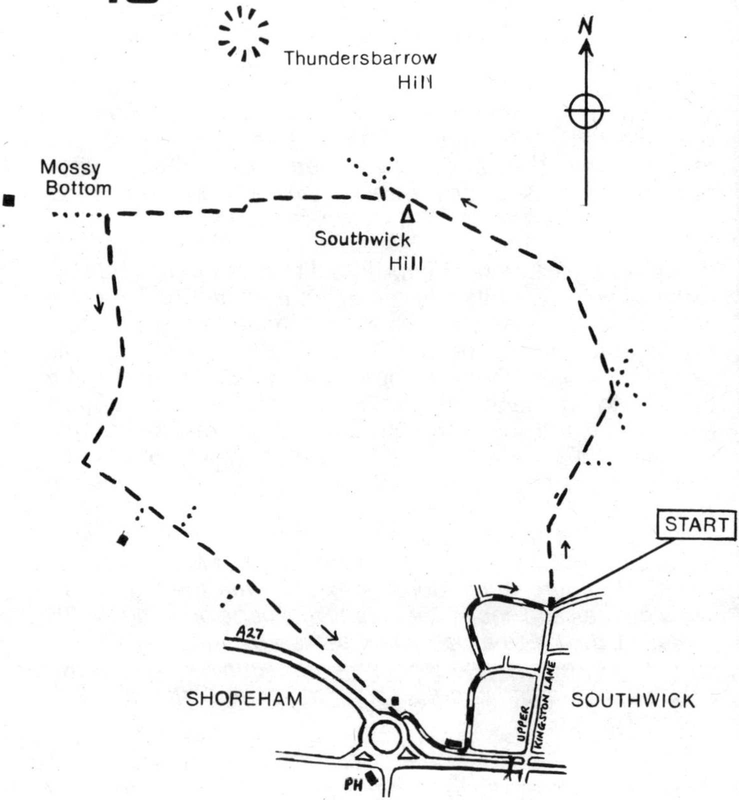

Thundersbarrow Hill
N
Mossy Bottom
Southwick Hill
START
A27
SHOREHAM
SOUTHWICK
UPPER KINGSTON LANE
PH

Walk 18

SOUTHWICK HILL

Southwick — Southwick Hill — Mossy Bottom — Holmbush Farm — Kingston Broadway — Southwick

Distance 4 mls **Climbing** 300 ft **Highest point** 396 ft

Starting point The rough parking area just beyond the northern end of Upper Kingston Lane, on the Southwick-Shoreham border (map reference TQ 238066).

A very short and easy ramble on the downs north of Shoreham, offering good views of the sea and the coastal plain. The early part can be extremely muddy in winter, due to the passage of horses on the same path.

Start off along the broad track leading north on to the downs, and make height steadily until in ¼ mile you can pause for a moment on a mysterious but conveniently placed sandstone block L, known locally as 'Rest and be Thankful'.

The southward view embraces most of Kingston Buci, New Shoreham and South Lancing. The down nearest to the built up area is Slonk Hill, said to have been the site of a fight to the death between the ancient Britons and the invading Saxons in the fifth century AD. Beyond lies Lancing Clump, and to the north-west are Thundersbarrow and gorse-topped Southwick Hill.

Continue uphill along the same track, which soon enters an area of sandy soil. For the next ¾ mile, alas, the going is often rendered muddy in wet weather by the passage of horses from the local riding school, and you may be forced to seek an alternative route through the gorse. You are now in National Trust territory, part of 596 acres of downland given to the Trust by West Sussex County Council in 1946. Keep on the ridge-top path (or as near to it as you can), ignoring the several paths descending to the R. About 20 yards before you emerge on to open downland you will come across the summit trig point L of Southwick Hill, the highest point of your walk at 396 feet.

Notice the bulky shape of Thundersbarrow Hill only ½ mile away to the north, and to its R the more distant Truleigh (with the masts), Edburton, Perching, and Dyke Hills — all 'peaks' along the South Downs Way.

WALKS 18 AND 19 DIVERGE HERE.

Turn L on emerging from the scrub, and almost immediately go R along a path heading west, parallel with the coast. This proves to be a gentle switchback across north-south valleys, and affords panoramic views of the coast. Over a hummock, distant Chanctonbury Ring comes into sight, with the east side of Mill Hill and the barns at Mossy Bottom less than ½ mile away. Just after the barns disappear again behind another rise, take a bridleway L, heading south in the direction of Slonk Hill. This passes along the eastern lip of a broad valley filled by one large field. When the field ends, turn L to take a south-east course along the west side of another field, with a riding stables in the valley R. Eventually your path merges with a rough track from these stables.

As you go, you will gradually become aware of the sound of traffic on the Brighton-bound trunk road. Pass the flint-built Holmbush farmhouse L, and just before reaching the roundabout, take the road L which makes for the parade of shops at Kingston Broadway. Now turn L up Hawkins Road and in 300 yards L again into Hawkins Crescent, which will take you back to Upper Kingston Lane, close to your starting point, L.

Walk 19

SOUTH DOWNS WAY TO DYKE HILL

Southwick — Southwick Hill — Thundersbarrow Hill — Beeding Hill — Truleigh Hill — Edburton Hill — Perching Hill — Fulking Hill — Dyke Hill — Fulking Hill — Cockroost Hill — Mile Oak Barn — Southwick Hill — Southwick

Distance 11 mls **Climbing** 1400 ft **Highest point** 711 ft

Starting point The rough parking area just beyond the northern end of Upper Kingston Lane, on the Southwick-Shoreham border (map reference TQ 238066).

Highlight of this energetic walk is a 4 mile section of the South Downs Way, passing over some of its loftier summits and culminating in a visit to the great rectangular Iron Age hillfort on Dyke Hill. There is plenty of climbing, but the paths are mostly firm and all are easily followed.

Follow Walk 18 as far as the trig point on Southwick Hill. The hill to the north-west is Thundersbarrow, at 491 feet the highest point in Shoreham, and you reach it in ½ mile by continuing along the same steadily rising path. Notice that its summit is crowned by a hillfort dating from about 500 BC, which was excavated in 1985. As you pursue the path northward, the hills along the South Downs Way line the horizon ahead — Beeding, Truleigh, Perching, Fulking and Dyke Hills, all of which you are about to conquer.

About ½ mile beyond Thundersbarrow turn L along a distinct bridleway descending into a valley and climbing out the other side. After 1¼ miles this will bring you to the motorists' viewpoint just below the top of Beeding Hill, at a 6-fingered signpost erected by the Society of Sussex Downsmen in 1973. The extensive view is described in Walk 12.

Now walk north-east along the South Downs Way as it runs adjacent to a high, surfaced lane as far as an avenue of conifers leading to the Truleigh Hill youth hostel L. After this,

19

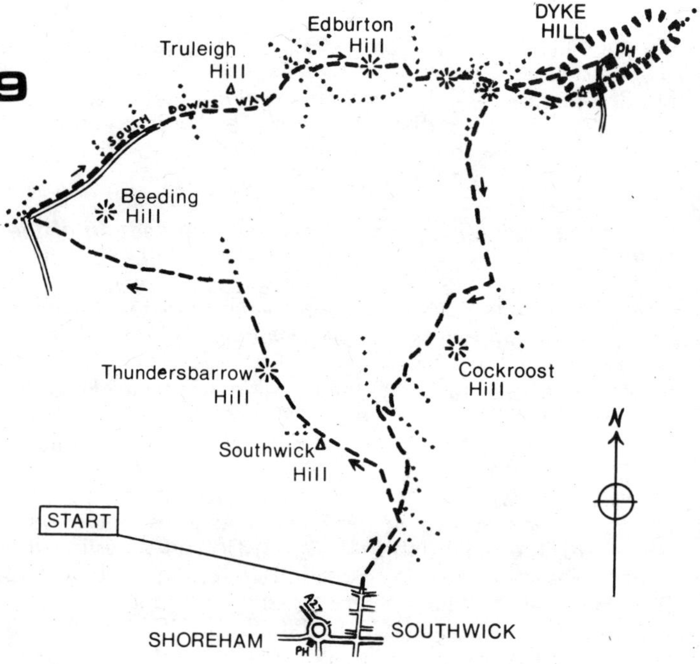
DYKE HILL
PH
Edburton Hill
Truleigh Hill
SOUTH DOWNS WAY
Beeding Hill
Thundersbarrow Hill
Cockroost Hill
Southwick Hill
N
START
A27
SHOREHAM
PH
SOUTHWICK

pass some houses L, close to the summit of Truleigh Hill (708 feet), and descend along the Way to a point where a bostal path drops steeply down the north side of the downs. In a further 100 yards you have a choice. You may continue along the well-defined South Downs Way or, if you have a sense of adventure, miss out the next ¾ mile by going through the small wooden gate L. Do not follow the signposted paths, but instead keep the wire fence R and ascend over well-grazed turf to the summit of Edburton Hill, at 600 feet. This is an exciting climb with an almost sheer drop L to the tiny hamlet of Edburton, and at the top there are a medieval motte and bailey and a superb view of the Wealden villages and the downs to the east, as far as Wolstonbury.

Cross a stile to the east of the summit and descend steeply, keeping the fence still R. Near a tall pylon rejoin the South Downs Way and continue along the chalky track as it ascends Perching Hill (590 feet) and later passes just north of the top of Fulking Hill (658 feet). After going through the smaller of a pair of gates you will observe ahead the huge promontory hillfort of Dyke Hill. Keep to the South Downs Way until it is about to pass the high ramparts of the earthwork, and then ascend them to attain the trig point on the summit, at 711 feet. Pause to take in the panorama to the south, embracing some fine golf courses and the built-up coastal plain. Walk east along the top of the rampart, cross a stile to a road, and turn L to reach the popular pub, restaurant and cafeteria. On their north side you will find a plaque on a stone pillar, to help you to identify landmarks in the Wealden jigsaw puzzle at your feet.

After a rest, or an exploration of the impressive hillfort, turn to the west, where the downland summits rise sharply from the Weald. Cross a stile, return westward across the ramparts and go through the gate encountered earlier. In a further 10 yards, fork L to pass close to the summit of Fulking Hill and descend gradually between fields. In ½ mile pass through a gate L and take a straight bridleway proceeding due south.

In a further ½ mile take a path R leaving at right-angles and pass round the north side of Cockroost Hill. Soon this veers south-west beside a transmission tower and begins to descend more rapidly, passing a dewpond R, into the bottom of a valley at the foot of Southwick Hill. Just before reaching

Mile Oak Barn, pass through one of another pair of gates, turn R, pass a tall pylon L, and at once go through an iron gate L to enter a sometimes muddy field. Now proceed under the transmission lines along a path which winds and ascends the east side of Southwick Hill. After passing under 3 more lines of electricity wires you will arrive at a stile. Cross it, and you are on the bridleway used for your outward journey. Turn L and descend steadily back to Upper Kingston Lane.

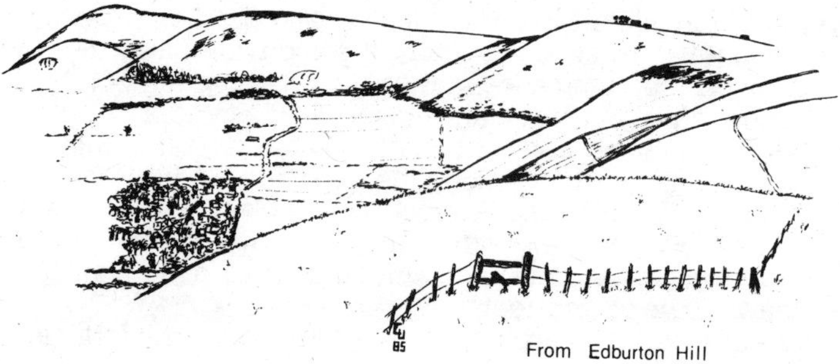

From Edburton Hill

Walk 20

MOUNT ZION

Portslade — Mile Oak Farm — Cockroost Hill — Mount Zion — Foredown Hill — Portslade

Distance 5 mls **Climbing** 450 ft **Highest point** 430 ft

Starting point The public car park in South Street, Portslade village, next to the Baptist church (map reference TQ 254063).

A short, easy stroll on the downs behind Portslade.

From the car park, go L and follow South Street as it passes 2 pubs, R. Then turn R into Valley Road and take the next turning L, which climbs steeply and becomes a rough track emerging in Mile Oak Road. Now turn R, and about 300 yards along this road take the footpath L leading around the backs of the houses on the north side of Brasslands Drive. After passing the last house L, turn R along a footpath, and R again just before the unsightly transmission towers.

Now walk north, noting the extensive view which embraces Worthing pier, Highdown Hill, Lancing Clump and Cissbury Ring (west), Southwick Hill (north) and Shoreham Harbour and Southwick (south). On arriving at the National Trust property of Southwick Hill, cross a stile and descend the hillside, keeping the fence on your R. Truleigh Hill appears on the skyline ahead, with Southwick and Cockroost Hills closer on either side. Just after passing beneath a tall transmission tower pass over one of the many stiles in the fence R, and continue to walk north with the backs of the Mile Oak houses R.

On reaching the corner of a field with farm buildings beyond the field ahead, descend R to a surfaced road, turn L to pass a pumping station R and enter Mile Oak Farm. The road has now become a farm track. Keep going until you arrive at a flint cattle shed L, and then take a path leading from a pair of gates R, upward around the north side of Cockroost Hill. At the highest point of this track it bears R beside yet

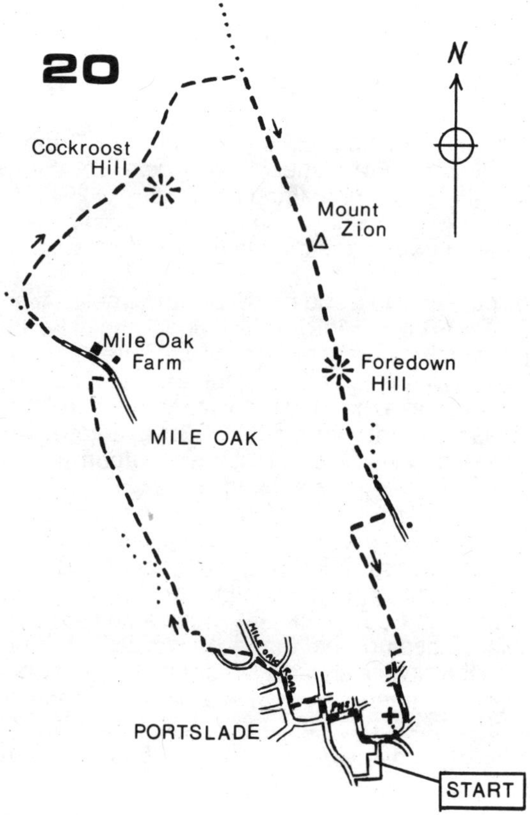
20
N
Cockroost Hill
Mount Zion
Mile Oak Farm
Foredown Hill
MILE OAK
PORTSLADE
START

another pylon, and 1 mile after leaving Mile Oak Farm arrives on the bridleway linking Portslade with the South Downs Way. Turn R and walk south along this well-defined track, passing in a further ½ mile the trig point at the summit of Mount Zion (399 feet).

The best view is northward over the rolling downs to Truleigh and Dyke Hills, and westward to the long ridge which includes Southwick Hill and Thundersbarrow. In the east, Hollingbury and Whitehawk Hill are distinctive on the horizon, but the southern aspect is a depressing one of the heavily built-up coastal plain, with the skyscrapers of Brighton and the power station at Shoreham Harbour only too prominent.

Continue along the same track over Foredown Hill (350 feet), but about 100 yards before it passes a conspicuous brick water tower L, take a footpath R, heading west towards Upper Portslade. Just before reaching the bungalows, turn L to resume your southward direction, along a path behind the back gardens. Keep on the same path for ⅓ mile, and emerge at length at a road junction. Cross over, and go down Manor Road. At the next junction, turn R, and visit if you can the parish church of St Nicolas, dating back to the 12th century. Then turn R again down South Street to the car park where your walk started.

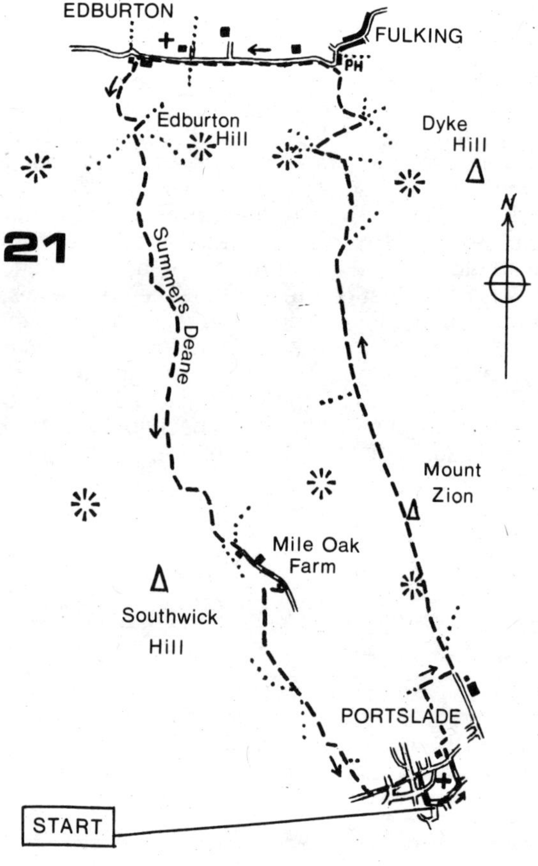
EDBURTON
FULKING
PH
Edburton Hill
Dyke Hill
21
N
Summers Deane
Mount Zion
Mile Oak Farm
Southwick Hill
PORTSLADE
START

Walk 21

FULKING AND EDBURTON

Portslade — Foredown Hill — Mount Zion — Fulking — Edburton — Summers Deane — Mile Oak Farm — Portslade

Distance 10 mls **Climbing** 950 ft **Highest point** 575 ft

Starting point The public car park in South Street, Portslade village, next to the Baptist church (map reference TQ 254063).

The outward route is along a high downland ridge, after which a steep descent leads to two picturesque but very different hamlets, nestling beneath the northern escarpment. The return is a strenuous climb followed by a ramble through one of the quietest and loveliest valleys in the downs.

Walk east along South Street, and turn L into Manor Road. Soon after passing the parish church go L again, and follow Manor Road up to its junction with Foredown Road. Cross the road to take the lane beside the primary school L, and continue north when the lane declines into a narrow path between hedges. In 100 yards this path bends to the R, but a few yards farther on resumes its northward course. Keep on it for about 1/3 mile, and on reaching the last bungalow turn R to climb steadily and emerge on a made-up road close to a large water tower.

Now turn L to pursue this lane as it deteriorates into a bridleway leading over the modest summits of Foredown Hill (350 feet) and Mount Zion (399 feet), which has a white trig point R beside the path. The view from here is described in Walk 20. Carry on walking north along this straight bridleway for a further 1¼ miles. On arriving at a signpost, turn R along a bridleway heading for the top of Fulking Hill, but after only 20 yards take a footpath L, resuming the northward direction, and culminating in a junction with the South Downs Way, where there is the usual grand view over the Weald.

Descend L along the Way for about 200 yards, and at the lowest point of the path leave it by a footpath R which heads down the hillside steeply as a deep, chalky, bostal track. In summer the banks on either side are rich in downland flora. Straight ahead lies the village of Poynings, overlooked by Newtimber Hill. About halfway down the hill turn L along a narrower path and double back to the west as you continue the steep descent into a semicircular coombe which has Fulking village at its mouth. Follow the same path into the scrub, and then head north until you are only 50 yards or so from the first house. Here you must veer L into the attractive streamside garden of the much-loved Sussex pub, the Shepherd and Dog.

Outside the pub, the stream which waters its garden, fed by fresh, clear, spring water from the downs, gushes forth beside an obsolete brick fountain by the roadside, and heads north to irrigate the Weald before helping to swell the Adur river. There are some pretty cottages in Fulking, along the lane leading past the pub.

Leaving Fulking by taking the road heading west, pass Perching Manor Farm R, with its duck pond and early Georgian manor house, and in 1 mile arrive at Edburton — just a few farms and a solid Sussex church.

Dedicated to St Andrew, the church dates mainly from the 13th century. Simple in style, its chief treasure is one of the 3 surviving leaden fonts in the county.

After another 300 yards along the road turn L up the track in front of September Cottage. Within another 60 yards find some wooden steps R and clamber up the bank as you follow a footpath ascending the west side of yet another coombe, first through some young scrub and later over open down. Continue along the same path when it ascends eastward to join a bridleway, and then turn R for 50 yards before arriving via a small gate on the South Downs Way. Edburton Hill is L, and Truleigh Hill (with the masts) R.

Cross the Way and now go southward into the peaceful valley of Summers Deane, with the gorse-clad slopes of Southwick Hill in the distance ahead. The route is well defined for the next 2½ miles as far as Mile Oak Farm, as it keeps close to the bottom of this winding valley all the way, except for a slight rise on the R side just after a group of trees.

Shortly before Mile Oak Farm, go L near a large pylon and pass a low flint cattle shed R. Carry on past the farm and pumping station L, and after the house and bungalow R find a footpath R. Climb steadily as far as the last back garden L, and then turn L to walk beside the boundary hedges and fences of properties in Mile Oak Road, with the high ridge R of Southwick Hill, a National Trust area.

After passing beneath a tall transmission tower, climb gently and leave the National Trust land by a stile. Keep going south with a thorn hedge L. On arriving at a playing field go L for a few yards before resuming your southerly course to arrive in Mile Oak Gardens in a further ¼ mile. Then turn L, cross Mile Oak Road and take a track opposite which will lead you down to Valley Road. Cross this also, and go down Drove Road to the former brewery at the foot of the hill. Now go R and emerge in South Street, close to your starting point.

Fulking

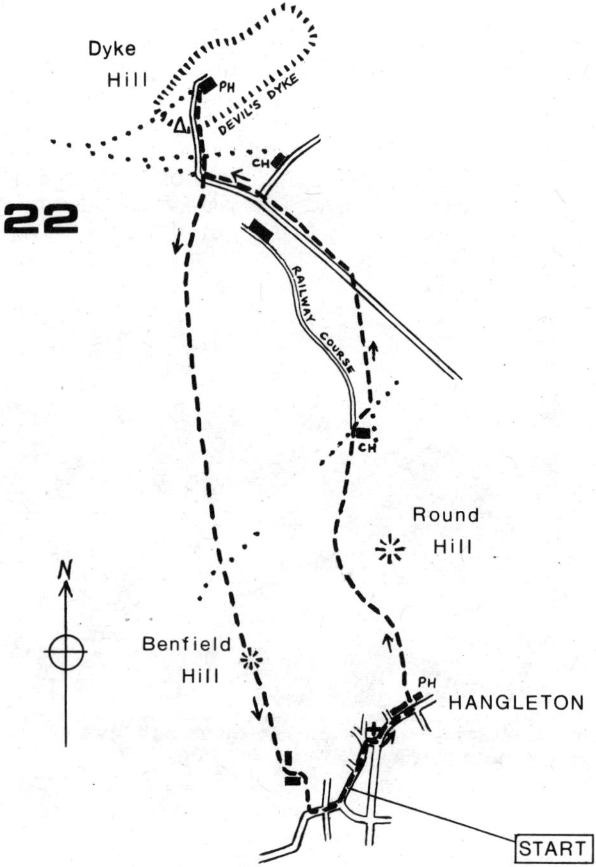
Dyke
Hill
PH
DEVIL'S DYKE
CH
22
RAILWAY
COURSE
CH
Round
Hill
N
Benfield
Hill
PH
HANGLETON
START

Walk 22

THE DYKE RAILWAY

Hangleton — Dyke Railway route — Dyke Hill — Benfield Hill — Hangleton

Distance 6 mls **Climbing** 600 ft **Highest point** 711 ft

Starting point In either St Helen's Drive or Hangleton Way, the roads on either side of the large green south of Hangleton parish church (map reference TQ 267072).

The Dyke railway was a branch line which between 1887 and 1938 left the main south coast railway at Aldrington and wound its way through Hove and on to the open downs, terminating at a point 500 feet above sea level, just short of the summit of Dyke Hill. The track is now but a memory, but its course is still traceable. Part of the route across the downs is now a public walkway, and is used for the first section of this ramble. The walk is therefore of particular interest to devotees of transport history, but it will be enjoyed also by those who appreciate an easy ramble on firm ground and gentle gradients, with a superb view from an important hillfort for good measure.

Walk northward past the green and St Helen's church L until you get to a parade of shops, also L. Now set off along the railway route, which begins between the shops and The Downsman public house. Almost at once a view unfolds of the downs as far as Truleigh Hill, and of the course of the old railway, running on ahead around the west side of Hangleton Round Hill.

Stay on the track for just over a mile, and when it is crossed by a path from the valley L, bear R up the hill, towards the white, single-storey clubhouse of the Brighton and Hove Golf Club. About 50 yards further on, turn L opposite the clubhouse, along a bridleway going north. In less than ½ mile you will arrive at the road from Brighton. Cross it, and walk L along the grassy area on the east side of the road. Soon you will notice a collection of farm buildings in the valley L. These stand on the site of the railway's former terminus, which was about 200 feet below the level of the summit — the principal reason why the railway lost business to motor traffic and had to close in 1938.

Cross the road going R to the clubhouse of the Dyke golf course and continue uphill on the path alongside the road to the summit. After crossing the South Downs Way, you will pass the Devil's Dyke R, a deep, waterless ravine, said to have been cut into the downs by the Devil, in an attempt to let in the sea to flood the churches of the Weald. From 1894 to 1909 an aerial cableway supported by 2 iron towers gave visitors a sensational ride across the ravine. Just beyond the Dyke you will come to the public house, restaurant and cafeteria overlooking one of the best known and most extensive views in Sussex.

Look for the viewpoint indicator by the large stone seat to pick out the features visible on a clear day. In particular, notice the precipitous north slopes of the downs running away to the west — Fulking, Perching, Edburton and Truleigh Hills and Tottington Mount. The flat-topped summit of Dyke Hill is a massive, rectangular Iron Age hillfort, one of the largest on the South Downs. Its circumference of nearly 1 mile is formed by a high rampart for some of the way, but in places the steepness of the hillside was sufficient defence from intruders. The highest point at 711 feet, marked by a triangulation pillar on the rampart west of the approach road, is a good vantage point to pick out your outward and return routes.

Leave Dyke Hill and retrace your steps past the Dyke to the sharp L bend in the road. Here take the bridleway leaving the road through an iron gate and head southward along a high ridge with fields on each side. Observe the line of the old railway L. After 2 miles enter the West Hove golf course, which covers the top of Benfield Hill.

Now continue south, straight across the golf course, until you pass a line of bushes L and pick up a track into Benfield Farm. There turn L in front of the terraced farm cottages and almost immediately go R. In a further 150 yards go L on reaching Hangleton Lane, cross Hangleton Valley Drive and arrive once more by the green where you started the walk.

Do not miss a visit to Hangleton church before leaving. It is a plain little building of flint construction, incorporating both Norman and Early English architecture, and was standing on its hillside site about 900 years before any of the surrounding development was dreamed of.

Dyke Railway

23

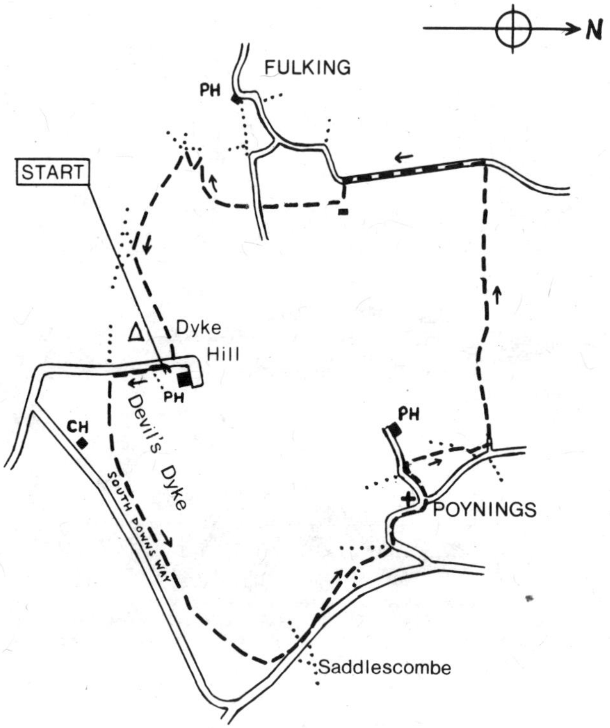
N
FULKING
PH
START
Dyke
Hill
PH
Devil's
Dyke
CH
SOUTH DOWNS WAY
PH
POYNINGS
Saddlescombe

Walk 23
POYNINGS

Dyke Hill — Saddlescombe — Poynings — Fulking — Dyke Hill

Distance 5 mls **Climbing** 550 ft **Highest point** 700 ft

Starting point The car park immediately south of the Devil's Dyke Hotel (map reference TQ 258109).

A short but exhilarating walk which is unusual in that the start is the highest point! Some parts can be muddy, but otherwise the route is a pleasant one, visiting a magnificent downland church and ending with a fine, exposed climb up the precipitous northern scarp.

Turn L on leaving the car park, pass the Devil's Dyke L, and 30 yards farther on take a bridleway L, signposted 'South Downs Way'. Follow this as it descends very gradually through the gorse and patches of bramble bush, keeping fairly close to the lip of the Dyke. When you emerge from the scrub after about ½ mile observe Newtimber Hill ahead, with Saddlescombe in the hollow below it and L the square flint tower of Poynings church.

Pass a downland reservoir surrounded by iron railings R, and continue the descent to Saddlescombe. Then turn L along the road, passing the 2 entrances to this tiny hamlet R, and then pick up a bridleway L which enters the bushes and proceeds due north. In wet weather parts of this can be very sticky, but it can be avoided by keeping to the longer route by road into Poynings. The bridleway emerges on the same road: go L along it to visit the delightful church of Holy Trinity.

This was built in the 14th century. A grey, flint, cruciform building, it stands solidly atop a small hillock overlooking the Weald. The interior is a surprise: there is an impression of lightness and space, with large, clear windows and tall, graceful pillars and arches.

At the road junction turn L, cross the road and go up some

paved steps to pass through an archway leading on to 'Cora's Walk'. In about 100 yards, just after a descent to cross a stream, go through a kissing gate R and take a path which keeps close to a high fence R. Stay alongside this as it bends R, but when it ends turn L to walk north beside a chestnut fence until you emerge in concrete-surfaced Mill Lane.

Now walk L past the attractive, white, mill house L. When the track ends by a sewage plant R, continue your westward direction along a path with a running stream L. After a further 150 yards cross a small footbridge over the stream and just beyond the corner of the field L go over a stile. Shortly after this pass through a gate and climb a small rise, noting the fine views of Wolstonbury and Newtimber Hills in the east, and the high, downland range to the south. L to R the summits are Dyke, Fulking, Perching, Edburton and Truleigh Hills.

Continue to walk west over the highest ground as you cross the middle of a very large field which is often cultivated. Beyond another stile proceed in the same direction, with a wood R and some glasshouses L, until you arrive by way of a further stile in Clappers Lane. Turn L and pass Hillbrook Nursery as you now walk south. At a R bend, follow the lane if you wish to visit the famous Shepherd and Dog inn at Fulking; otherwise turn L along a bridleway to the cricket ground, and just before its entrance bear R along another muddy track which in ¼ mile will bring you to the Poynings-Fulking road.

Cross the road and continue southward towards the base of the downs. In about 200 yards fork R to take a footpath which begins the climb through trees. Just after emerging on to open down the path swings L, and 100 yards further on it bends R again. At a crosspaths turn L up the chalky path around the hillside, pausing to take in the dramatic western view of the slopes of Edburton and Truleigh Hills, dropping sheer to the Weald.

Now by a narrow path hugging the hillside climb steadily towards the hotel and tree clump on the summit of Dyke Hill. A small wooden gate near the top of the ridge leads on to the close-cropped grassland surrounding the large, rectangular Iron Age hillfort. Pass over the high ramparts and make for the hotel, which is just north of your starting point.

Walk 24

DEVIL'S DYKE AND WOLSTONBURY

Dyke Hill — Devil's Dyke — Poynings — Newtimber — Wolstonbury Hill — Pyecombe — Newtimber Hill — Saddlescombe — Summer Down — Dyke Hill

Distance 8½ mls **Climbing** 1200 ft **Highest point** 700 ft

Starting point The car park immediately south of the Devil's Dyke Hotel (map reference TQ 258109).

The view from Wolstonbury is one of the finest and most extensive on all the Sussex downs. In this walk the ascent of this isolated hill, crowned with an Iron Age hillfort, is combined with a stroll through that curious phenomenon, the Devil's Dyke. There is plenty of climbing, and plenty of mud in winter.

Go through the gap in the bank at the south-east corner of the car park, and descend steeply into the bottom of the Devil's Dyke, a deep, waterless cleft in the downs, on the southern side of the great hillfort surmounting Dyke Hill. Now walk eastward along the green path through the Dyke, whose slopes rise 300 ft to either side. As you walk, the round shape of Newtimber Hill appears ahead.

Just after the path veers north and enters some scrub, cross a small stream and continue to head north along a gently rising path through the trees just to the R of the valley bottom. When you leave the wood the square, flint tower of Poynings church appears on the skyline. Soon the sometimes muddy path emerges on a road, and you must turn L along it to visit the lovely parish church of Holy Trinity, described in Walk 23.

Now take the road opposite the north transept, signposted to Pyecombe, and pass a building L with a white clock tower. Almost at once find a footpath R into a school playground, cross a stile behind the school and continue east with a hedge L. Cross a stream by a wooden footbridge and carry on walking east across a field. Then go through a gate, and make

24

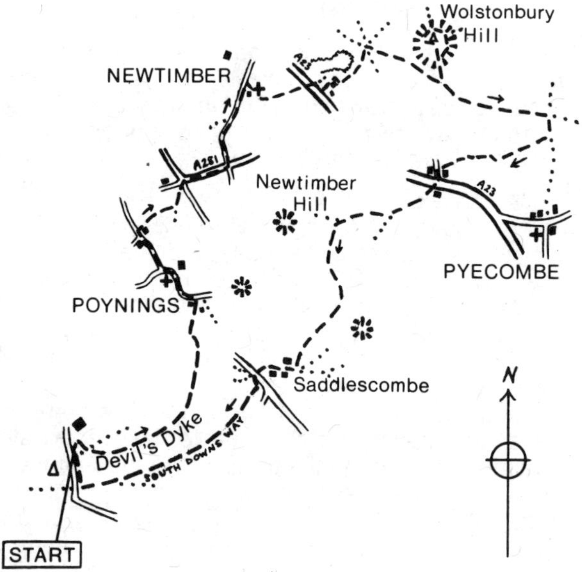
Wolstonbury
Hill
NEWTIMBER
A23
A281
Newtimber
Hill
A23
PYECOMBE
POYNINGS
Saddlescombe
N
Devil's Dyke
SOUTH DOWNS WAY
START

for another gate in the north-east corner of the next field, near some isolated houses (if the field is ploughed you may have to keep to its edge). Look back for a superb view of the western downs, embracing from east to west Dyke, Fulking, Perching, Edburton and Truleigh Hills, and then the downs beyond the Adur culminating in Chanctonbury, with its crown of beeches.

From the roundabout beyond this gate take the road opposite, signposted A281 Brighton. Wolstonbury is now on the horizon. In ¼ mile turn L to walk along a lane into the tiny hamlet of Newtimber. The church, R, is set in one of the most beautiful and secluded of Sussex churchyards.

Dedicated to St John the Baptist, Newtimber church was built in the 13th century by the lord of the Manor, who resided in nearby Newtimber Place. The tower was added in 1839. It is a simple little building with a solitary transept, and is somewhat darkened by its stained glass windows.

Follow the footpath leading from the south side of the church, turn L after crossing a stile and walk along the north side of a field. At its end climb over another stile and now make straight for the busy Brighton-London trunk road, which you will join just R of a low, flint wall. Cross the road with extreme care.

Do not take the chalk track straight ahead, but find a footpath about 20 yards to the south. Keep a large barn R, walk around the back of it and then find a stile leading on to a path which climbs eastward past a chalk quarry behind the trees L and up the east end of a narrow coombe. After going over a stile at the top go L for 10 yards and emerge through a gate on to open downland. Now go R and, keeping a fence close R, walk up the rising ridge for nearly ½ mile. When the bridleway reaches its highest point take a footpath L, leading to the hillfort at the top of Wolstonbury Hill.

Within the Iron Age earthwork (unusual in that the rampart is constructed outside the ditch) are a dewpond, a number of bumps and hollows and a trig point at 677 feet. For a splendid all round view, go west to the edge of the rampart and walk around it in a clockwise direction. In the west Newtimber Hill is dominant in the foreground, while behind it stretches the downland range around Truleigh, and beyond lie Cissbury, Chanctonbury and the hills west of the Arun. Northward the red brick facade of Danny lies at your feet, and beyond you may discern the Wealden towns of Hurstpierpoint, Hassocks, Burgess Hill and Ditchling. To the east is the rounded form of Ditchling Beacon and nearer stand the distinctive shapes of Jack and Jill, the Clayton windmills. Southward, through a cleft in the downs, appear the tower blocks of Brighton.

Return to the bridleway you left earlier and turn L along it for about ½ mile. At a crosspaths just beyond a gate go R along another bridleway, but in 100 yards cross a stile R and climb the broad hill ahead. (If you wish to visit Pyecombe church continue along the bridleway and rejoin the route at Wayfield Farm by returning along the side of A23). After observing the view L to Pyecombe and back to Jack and Jill, start to descend south-west, cross a stile and bear R for a short distance to find and cross another stile in the bushes below. Now drop down diagonally across a field to a farm in the western half of Pyecombe village.

Emerge on a lane past some ancient cottages, cross A23 once more, and take a footpath opposite, leading up some stone steps and over a stile beside Wayfield Farm. Walk up the hill on either side of the hedgerow (whichever path is less muddy). At a wooden signpost continue uphill with the fence R, and shortly enter a wood by a small gate. Continue the ascent through and beyond the wood, and carry on to another small gate. Do not go through it, but turn L, keeping a wire fence and the top of Newtimber Hill R. The hamlet of Saddlescombe now lies in the hollow ahead,and you begin to descend towards it along a bridleway which winds in and out of a coombe. Just before arriving at the farm you can avoid the worst of the mud by climbing over a stile R and going down a short path to the farm cottages.

Now you are on the South Downs Way. Follow it through Saddlescombe, cross the road and resume the Way as it passes a reservoir L and makes the ascent of Summer Down, on the southern side of the Devil's Dyke. Just over a mile from Saddlescombe, when you arrive on the Dyke road, turn R to get back to your starting point in the car park, close to the hotel, cafeteria and toilets.

Walk 25

JACK AND JILL

Patcham — Sweet Hill — Haresdean — Pyecombe — Clayton windmills — Keymer Hill — Chattri — Patcham

Distance 8½ mls **Climbing** 850 ft **Highest point** 765 ft

Starting point The car park just off Mill Road, immediately west of the railway bridge, by the entrance lane to Patcham pumping station (map reference TQ 296092).

An easy ramble over the downs north of Brighton, visiting the hamlet of Pyecombe and the much loved Sussex landmarks, Jack and Jill windmills, on the South Downs Way above Clayton.

Walk for 50 yards along the pumping station lane, and at the first bend go straight on along the track which heads uphill, passing a reservoir R and another L, both surrounded by railings. Go through a metal gate and continue to ascend to the summit of Sweet Hill (424 feet), marked by a trig point beside the path, L.

The path continues in a north-westerly direction, levelling out and giving sight of the Clayton mills away to the north-east. When you have walked about 1½ miles from the car park, a view unfolds L towards the bush-cloaked downs around Dyke Hill. Just afterwards, bear R in front of a metal gate to resume the ascent along the obvious path. At a second gate bear R again, and next pass through a third gate, continuing with a good view R to Hollingbury and Brighton.

Once over the brow of the hill, Wolstonbury is the prominent down which comes into view L, with Pyecombe ahead. Within a few yards your path is joined from the L by the South Downs Way, which will form your route for the next 3 miles. Descend by its sometimes muddy track to the farm and riding stables at Haresdean, cross the busy London-Brighton trunk road, pass through the forecourt of the Plough Inn and turn up the narrow lane to Pyecombe church, L.

25

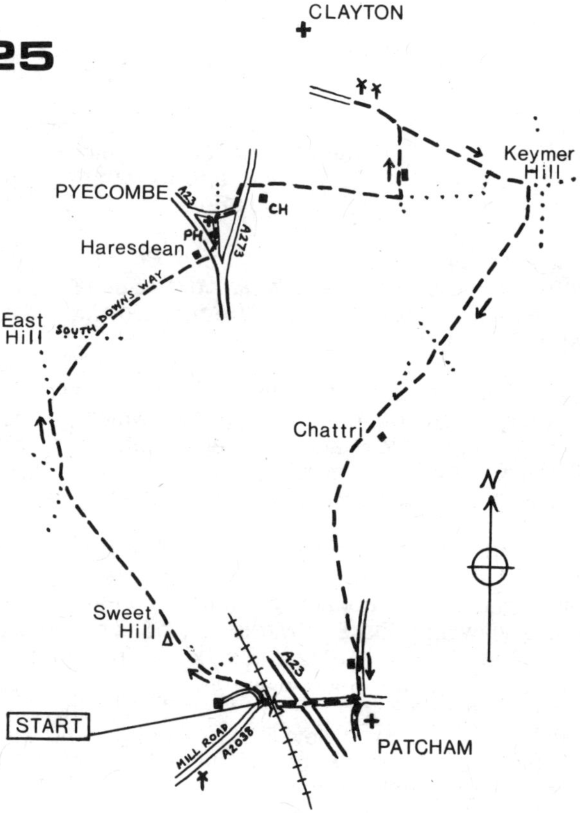

CLAYTON
Keymer
Hill
PYECOMBE
A23
CH
PH
Haresdean
A273
SOUTH DOWNS WAY
East
Hill
Chattri
N
Sweet
Hill
A23
START
MILL ROAD
A2038
PATCHAM

It's a small, simple church of flint, partially covered by pebbledash. Most of the fabric is Norman, but the tower, with its familiar 'Sussex cap' is later, dating from the 13th century. Its prize possession is a deep, cylindrical font of decorated lead — one of only 3 in Sussex which survived the Civil War.

Leaving the church, go east down Church Hill to the Burgess Hill road. Turn L to walk beside the roadside hedge for 150 yards, and then cross the road and go up the drive of the Pyecombe Golf Club. From the car park, follow the South Downs Way leading east on to the downs. Now go gently uphill with the superb golf course on either side. Just over ½ mile from the clubhouse pass through a gate across the Way, a few yards later turn L along the bridleway through New Barn Farm and next go L again to visit the windmills.

Jill mill, the farther west, is a typical, weatherboarded Sussex post mill. It was built early in the 19th century on a site near the Seven Dials in Brighton. Within 30 years the expanding town had encroached on to the downs surrounding the mill, taking the wind out of its sails. In 1852 it was sold to a new owner, who had it towed across the downs to its present windswept site, on a trolley dragged by horses and oxen. Jack, a brick tower mill, was erected in 1866 adjacent to the roundhouse of a post mill which it replaced. By 1908 both Jack and Jill had ceased to work, but the exterior of the tower mill received a facelift in 1973, when it secured the title role in the film 'The Black Mill'. The mills are now maintained in good repair, thanks to the efforts of the Jack and Jill Mills Preservation Society, and Jill is usually open to public on Sundays.

Leaving the windmills, walk eastward to retrace your steps as far as the lane from New Barn Farm. Then continue to go east on the South Downs Way for about ¾ mile, until just before the summit of Keymer Hill. Here take a bridleway R, going south across the fields, and keep on it all the way back to Patcham. About 1½ miles after Keymer Hill you will pass just above the white dome of The Chattri, L, a monument to Indian soldiers who gave their lives in the Great War.

Keep to the path as it begins to descend steadily on a ridge above the west side of a deep valley,and about a mile from The Chattri you will join the lane through the valley. Turn R, walk past a large farm R, and at the crossroads go straight on down Church Hill if you wish to visit the picturesque cottages and church of All Saints in Patcham village. If not, turn R to descend by Vale Avenue to the traffic lights on the London road. Cross here, and go under the railway bridge to regain your starting point.

Jill & Jack, 1905

Walk 26

DITCHLING AND THE BEACON

Stanmer — Lower Standean — Keymer Post — Ditchling — East End — Ditchling Beacon — Moon's Bottom — Stanmer

Distance 11 mls **Climbing** 1500 ft **Highest point** 813 ft

Starting point The car park in Stanmer village, just east of the pond by the church (map reference TQ 337096).

A hilly walk across unspoiled downland, taking in 2 short stretches of the South Downs Way, a visit to the picturesque village of Ditchling and the extensive view from Ditchling Beacon, highest point in East Sussex. The start is at Stanmer, a tiny village within the Brighton borough, set in beautiful parkland with a large manor house built early in the 18th century and a 19th century flint church notable for its graceful spire.

Leaving the car park turn R, pass the well house next to the church L, and turn R again, up the village street of flint cottages. Just after the last row turn L at a duckpond to walk up a quiet lane, signposted 'No Through Road'. In ¾ mile pass between the white Upper Lodges, and shortly afterwards bear R through a beechwood picnic area and R along the verge of the road between Brighton and Ditchling.

Stay on the road for just over ½ mile, with a view L of the open downs and the conspicuous white tower mill at Patcham. Immediately after passing under transmission lines cross a stile L and go down a footpath which leads at first westward and then swings north into a valley dominated by a large barn. Pass the barn L and go through a gate to continue the descent until you meet a road through the valley bottom. Turn R along this lane and walk right through the farm at Lower Standean. About 200 yards after the last farm building turn R on a path leading uphill in a northerly direction, with woods L and a field R. Continue north when

26

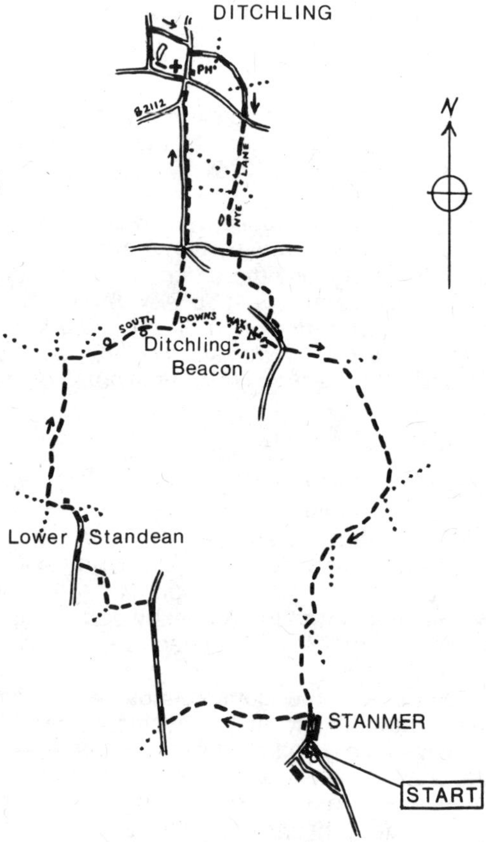
DITCHLING
PH
B2112
NYE LANE
N
SOUTH DOWNS WAY
Ditchling Beacon
Lower Standean
STANMER
START

the field ends, and eventually arrive on the South Downs Way at Keymer Post.

Turn R and walk eastward along the broad, grassy Way, passing 2 dried-up dewponds, L and R. Enter the fenced nature reserve of the Sussex Trust for Nature Conservation and immediately go L to cross a stile on the lip of the ridge. Now drop down the steep hillside, using a sometimes slippery grass path by a wire fence R. Observe below your objective, the lane leading north into Ditchling. Leave the grassland and after crossing a further stile continue the descent through scrub to emerge at length on the road mentioned earlier. Walk along its path right into Ditchling.

Pride of the village is the 13th century cruciform church of St Margaret, with its 'Sussex cap', set on a hill above an attractive green and lively pond. The main streets have many pleasing houses of various periods, and from most parts there are good views of the downland range, dominated by the Beacon.

At the crossroads in the centre of the village turn L and soon climb the steps R to the churchyard. Then go west across the well-tended green and turn R along the lane by the pond. Shortly afterwards turn R along Boddington's Lane (more a path than a lane), and follow it eastward for 200 yards until you arrive at a main road. Go R for about 20 yards, and turn L down East End Lane, which will take you past attractive cottages and houses of many ages and bring you to the Lewes Road opposite a petrol station.

Continue to walk south by crossing the road and proceeding down Nye Lane, which heads for the downs between hedgerows, changing its surface at frequent intervals from muddy path, to rough track, to white concrete, and back to mud. On arriving after ¾ mile on Underhill Lane turn L along the road for 100 yards and then R up a bridleway. This also can be muddy at times, but if you persevere as it winds and climbs its way around the hillside you will arrive ultimately at the car park just east of the summit of Ditchling Beacon. Walk round the south side of the car park to make the brief ascent to the trig point on the summit, at 813 feet.

The view from the summit is one of the best in East Sussex. In the west, Worthing can be seen on the coast, and to its R the downland peaks of tree-crowned Dyke Hill, Truleigh Hill with the masts, the familiar shape of Chanctonbury and much nearer Wolstonbury. In the Weald to the north the spire of Hurstpierpoint church is prominent, as are the communities of Hassocks, Keymer, Burgess Hill and Haywards Heath, with the hills of Surrey on the horizon. Ditchling is out of sight beneath your vantage point, but the church of Streat appears among the trees to the north-east. To the east, the downs roll on to Streat Hill and Blackcap, while in the distance stand rounded Windover Hill, the nose-like Firle Beacon and the wedged shape of Seaford Head, nearest the sea. In the south the downs around Newmarket Hill, the stands on Brighton racecourse and the chimneys of Southwick power station may all be discerned.

Return to the car park, and go through a small wooden gate to walk east along the South Downs Way for a further 600 yards. Then find a bridleway leading from another gate R, at first south-east in the direction of the white cliff of Seaford Head. Soon it veers south, and will take you into a shallow coombe and out the other side. About 300 yards from its base, go through a gate R and descend once more, into the remote and winding valley known as Moon's Bottom.

Walk through the valley for about ¼ mile, pass through another gate, and in a further 200 yards find a pair of gates R, on the edge of a wood. Beyond these, follow a path which climbs through the trees, and at the top go straignt on, along a chalky track which now descends steadily to arrive after a further mile back at your starting point by Stanmer Pond.

Stanmer

Walk 27

HOLLINGBURY AND THE WILD PARK

Ditchling Road — Hollingbury Castle — Moulsecoomb Wild Park — Hollingbury Castle — Upper Roedale — Ditchling Road

Distance 3 mls **Climbing** 490 ft **Highest point** 584 ft

Starting point The small car park just off the east side of Ditchling Road, Brighton, opposite Woodbourne Avenue (map reference TQ 316078).

A short but energetic walk around a piece of unexpected and delightful countryside in the middle of built-up Brighton. It includes a steep descent into the Wild Park and a moderately tough climb of Hollingbury.

Walk north along the verge beside Ditchling Road for about 300 yards until you reach a public footpath R. Follow this across the golf course until in 200 yards you see the ramparts L of an Iron Age hillfort, Hollingbury Castle. Head straight for the ramparts (being careful not to impede the golfers) and walk L along the top to the white triangulation pillar at 584 feet.

On a clear day several familiar hills line the western horizon: from R to L they are Wolstonbury, Newtimber Hill, Dyke Hill, Truleigh Hill, Chanctonbury, Cissbury and Highdown. When it is exceptionally clear you may discern Shanklin Down on the Isle of Wight, above and L of Worthing pier. Southward lies Brighton, dominated by the Racehill, while to the east are Cliffe Hill and Mount Caburn, beyond Lewes, and Newmarket Hill with its crowning mast.

Now continue east along the top of the embankment, noting the overgrown state of the centre of the 'Castle'. When the golf course L seems to end, take a path descending L off the rampart. Suddenly the golf course reappears, and you must pass along the edge of a fairway to the 12th tee. Then take the gravel path R through a small wood, pass the 11th

27

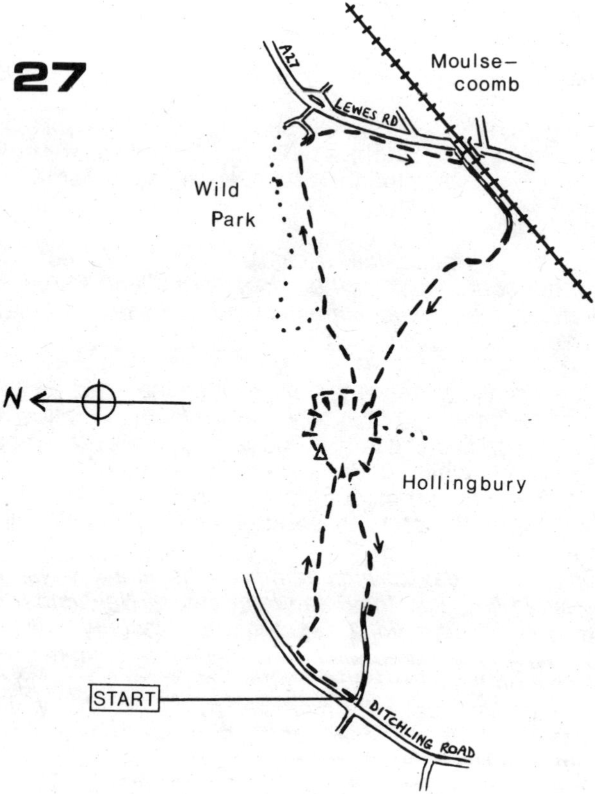

Moulse–
coomb
A27
LEWES RD
Wild
Park
N
Hollingbury
START
DITCHLING ROAD

green R and find a gap in the bushes L, where there is a seat overlooking the deep valley of Moulsecoomb Wild Park. Do not begin the descent here: it is much too steep to be safe. Instead, take the path R between the bushes, and in about 300 yards arrive at a cluster of timber posts near a clearing, which is where you must start the descent to the very bottom of the Park. Once there, take the nearest of 2 tracks through the valley and go R towards its mouth. Once in sight of the Brighton-Lewes road keep close to the hillside R, passing as you go a stone pillar R, commemorating the opening of the Wild Park on 30 June 1925.

Continue walking in the direction of the railway viaduct, pass a block of public toilets L and then pick up a track which leads uphill beside the railway line. When this bears R stay on it for a further 100 yards until it enters private property (a noisy dog kennels). Now enter a wood by the narrow path which climbs quite steeply, keeping the kennels fence L. When this veers L, take a R fork to continue through the wood. There is a maze of paths here, but if you take care to keep climbing all the time, in a general north-westerly direction, you will emerge once more in the scrub surrounding the summit of Hollingbury.

Cross the golf course to mount the southern rampart, and walk L along the top. Leave the embankment at its western side, and make your way across the fairway (again giving way to golfers). Pass beside a tall privet hedge L, go through a gap L at its end and make your way towards some farm buildings near an allotment site. Here you will find a surfaced lane which will take you through a small wood back to the car park.

28

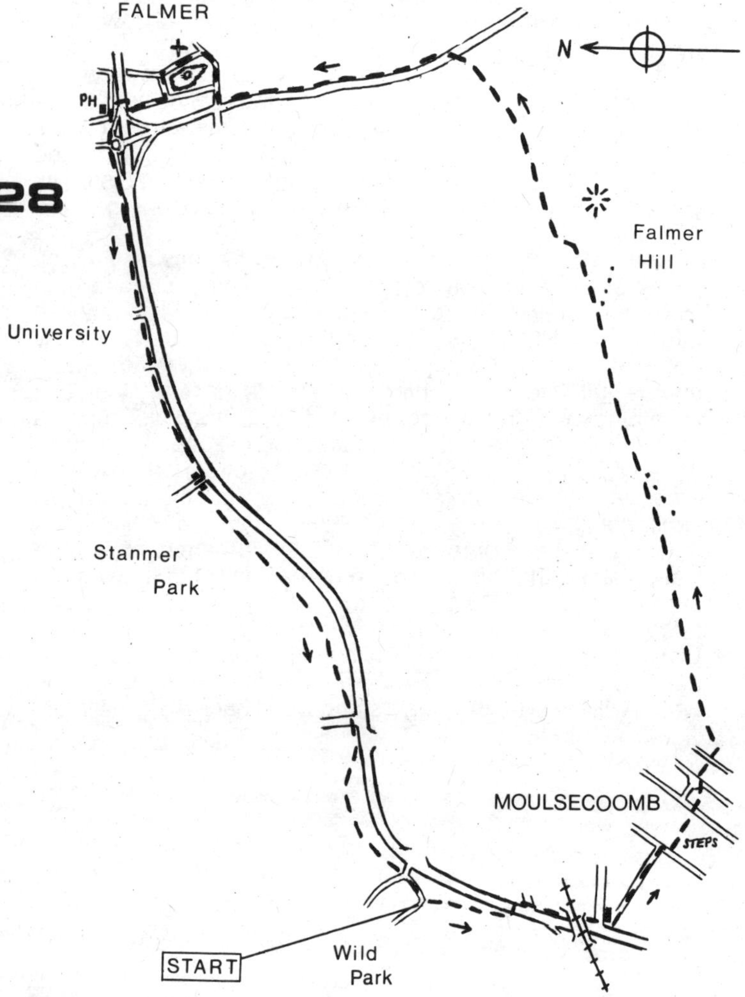

FALMER
N
PH
Falmer
Hill
University
Stanmer
Park
MOULSECOOMB
STEPS
START
Wild
Park

Walk 28
FALMER

Moulsecoomb Wild Park — Moulsecoomb — Falmer Hill — Falmer — Stanmer Park — Moulescoomb Wild Park

Distance 5 mls **Climbing** 390 ft **Highest point** 510 ft

Starting point The entrance to Moulsecoomb Wild Park from Lewes Road, Brighton (map reference TQ 332080). There is plenty of space to park on the grass beside the track along the south side.

An easy ramble over the downs behind Moulsecoomb to the attractive village of Falmer, with a return through the woodland of Stanmer Park.

Start off along the grass path going parallel with the road towards Brighton. Cross the road at the pedestrian-controlled lights and walk under the tall railway bridge. Just after the first turning L (Broadfields), go L behind the houses up a fairly steep lane, and turn R at the T-junction. Almost at once you will spot a flight of steps leading up through the tiers of houses which form the Moulsecoomb estate. Start up these steps, and climb nearly 200 feet, crossing 2 roads on the way, and after a third go up the sloping path between 2 houses to emerge at a field on the open downs. Turn L along a grass path, and follow it as it acquires a sheltering row of bushes on its R. Soon this develops into a wider track, leading over the top of Falmer Hill at just over 500 feet.

The western view is dominated by the bulky shape of Hollingbury Castle, a prehistoric hillfort in the centre of the built-up area. Beyond is a superb view across Brighton to the coastal strip extending to Worthing and even (on a very clear day) the Isle of Wight. As you continue along the track, note the view L across the valley to the slender spire of Stanmer church in the woods, the fine modern buildings of Sussex University and the square, flint tower of Falmer church.

After about 1¼ miles, the track joins the road from Rottingdean. Turn L along its verge and walk northward until you arrive at Park Street, which will lead you R past a farm to Falmer pond.

Falmer is a pleasant, secluded village of flint cottages clustered around a large pond which started life as a dewpond. The church was built in 1815 in the Norman style. Unfortunately the attractive southern part of the village is separated from the northern half by a deep cutting carrying the Brighton-Lewes road, the 2 halves being linked by a footbridge.

Leave the village green by Park Street, at its north-west corner, and at the flint wall go R and cross the footbridge to the Swan Inn, a Free House with real ale. Now take the tarmac path around the north side of a roundabout and then alongside the main road in the direction of Brighton, passing the entrance to Sussex University.

The University buildings, begun in 1960, were designed for their parkland setting by Sir Basil Spence, architect of Coventry cathedral, drawing inspiration on this occasion from the ruin of the Colosseum in Rome.

Continue along the same path until you reach the lodges guarding the way into Stanmer Park. Enter, and immediately turn L, to take a track skirting the edge of the sports ground. At the end of the grassed area follow a path into the woods, and walk parallel with the busy road until you emerge at the junction of Coldean Lane and the main road. Cross Coldean Lane, and resume the roadside path as now it passes through the edge of more delightful parkland to arrive back at the entrance to the Wild Park.

Walk 29
BLACKCAP

Falmer — St Mary's Farm — Streathill Farm — Plumpton Plain — Blackcap — Balmer Down — Newmarket Inn — Newmarket Plantation — Falmer

Distance 10½ mls **Climbing** 850 ft **Highest point** 677 ft

Starting point Beside the lane in front of Falmer church, by the pond (map reference TQ 355087).

A splendid downland walk along well-defined paths, incorporating extensive views over Weald and downs and more than 6 miles of the South Downs Way.

From Falmer pond walk north along East Street, and when the road ends at a flint wall go L along a footpath above the main road as far as a footbridge. Cross the bridge and turn R to pass the flint cottages of Middle Street. Then walk L up Ridge Road past the Old Forge Barn R. Keep going north until you reach a fork at Ridge Farm, where you must follow the surfaced lane which soon descends with a beechwood R. Enter the tranquil valley in which lies St Mary's Farm, with its tree-sheltered pond.

A few yards after passing the farm R, go L, to make a steady northward ascent. In ½ mile, at a small wood L, look back for a view to the stands at Brighton racecourse in the south and distant Firle Beacon to the east. Continue the slow climb past Streathill Farm with its conspicuous silo, and soon emerge on the ridge-top South Downs Way. Walk R along the Way, where very soon a view opens L across the Weald to the forest ridges and R to the downland block around Newmarket Hill.

For a pub lunch you will need to take the bostal path L down to Plumpton (don't forget about the ascent afterwards!), but otherwise go straight on over the barely discernable summit of Plumpton Plain (650 feet). Note the view L to Plumpton Agricultural College and in the distance the small, white shape of Chailey windmill. After a short and gentle

29

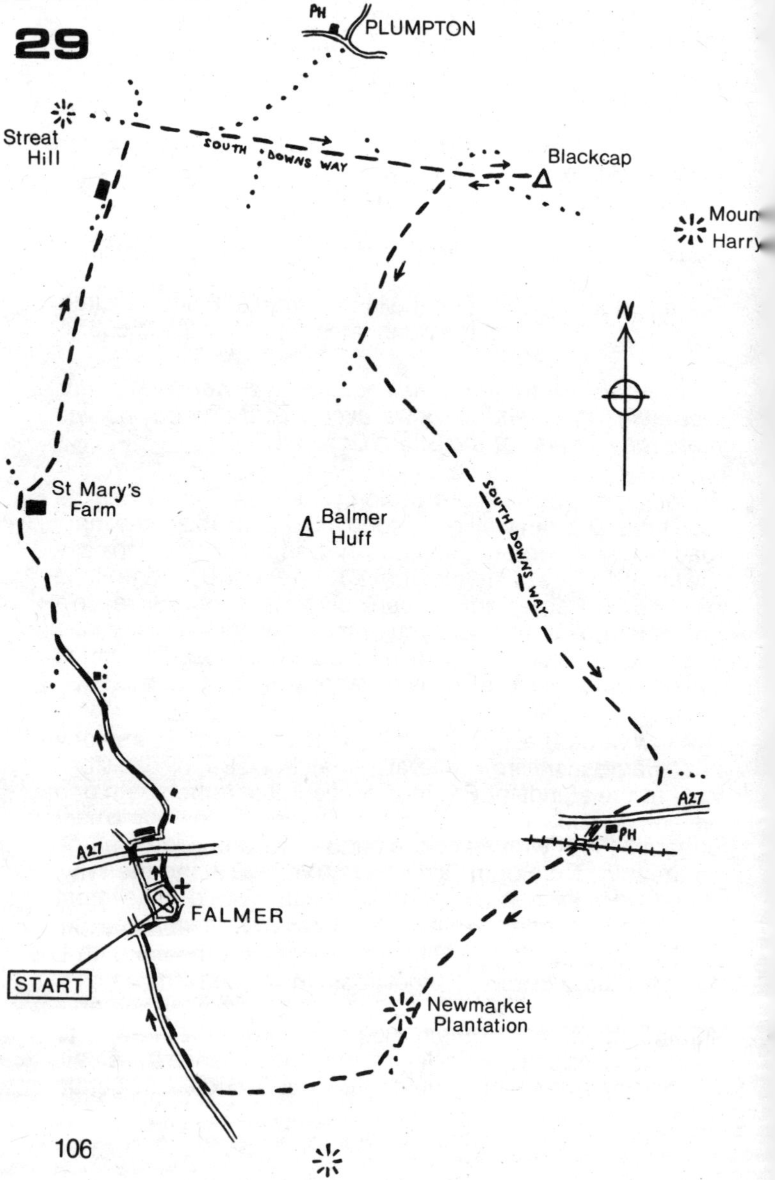

PH
PLUMPTON
Streat Hill
SOUTH DOWNS WAY
Blackcap
Mount Harry
N
St Mary's Farm
Balmer Huff
SOUTH DOWNS WAY
A27
PH
A27
FALMER
START
Newmarket Plantation

descent, make the brief climb to the trig point on Blackcap (677 feet) for a superb all round view.

To the east the green hill in the foreground is Mount Harry, on whose slopes was fought the Battle of Lewes in 1264; just behind it are Cliffe Hill and Mount Caburn, with Windover Hill and the nose-like promontory of Firle Beacon on the horizon. Notice Hamsey church, just L of Mount Harry. To the south-east are the broad valley of the Ouse and Seaford Head, L.

Descend Blackcap by the way you came, and after passing through a wooden gate turn L to pick up the South Downs Way again as it goes south along a broad ridge with a wood R. In just over ½ mile, about 100 yards before a line of transmission wires turn L along a track, again signposted 'South Downs Way'. Soon this passes under the wires and descends steadily along Balmer Down in the direction of the Ouse valley. After 1½ miles on this track, a few yards before a lonely barn L, cross a stile R and climb by a terraced path to another stile which leads into the corner of a wood.

At a crosspaths as you leave the wood, where the Brighton-Lewes road comes into view, go straight on (south-west) in the direction of a tree-topped summit. Now descend to cross the busy main road just before reaching the Newmarket pub. The South Downs Way now continues as a lane between the pub and a petrol station. Walk up it to pass under a railway bridge and bear R up the hill towards the tree clump, which is Newmarket Plantation. When you reach it, pause to admire the northward view to Blackcap, and to its R the stands of the former Lewes racecourse, the county town itself and attendant Mount Caburn.

Pass the Plantation and go through a gate R. Now double back for a few yards on the other side of the fence and pass through another gate before bearing L to walk along a path which winds its way down to the Falmer-Woodingdean road, above a deep valley called Loose Bottom. Falmer church appears to the north-west. On reaching the road turn R and walk along a path beside it as you descend towards Falmer. The village pond is reached by turning R along Park Street.

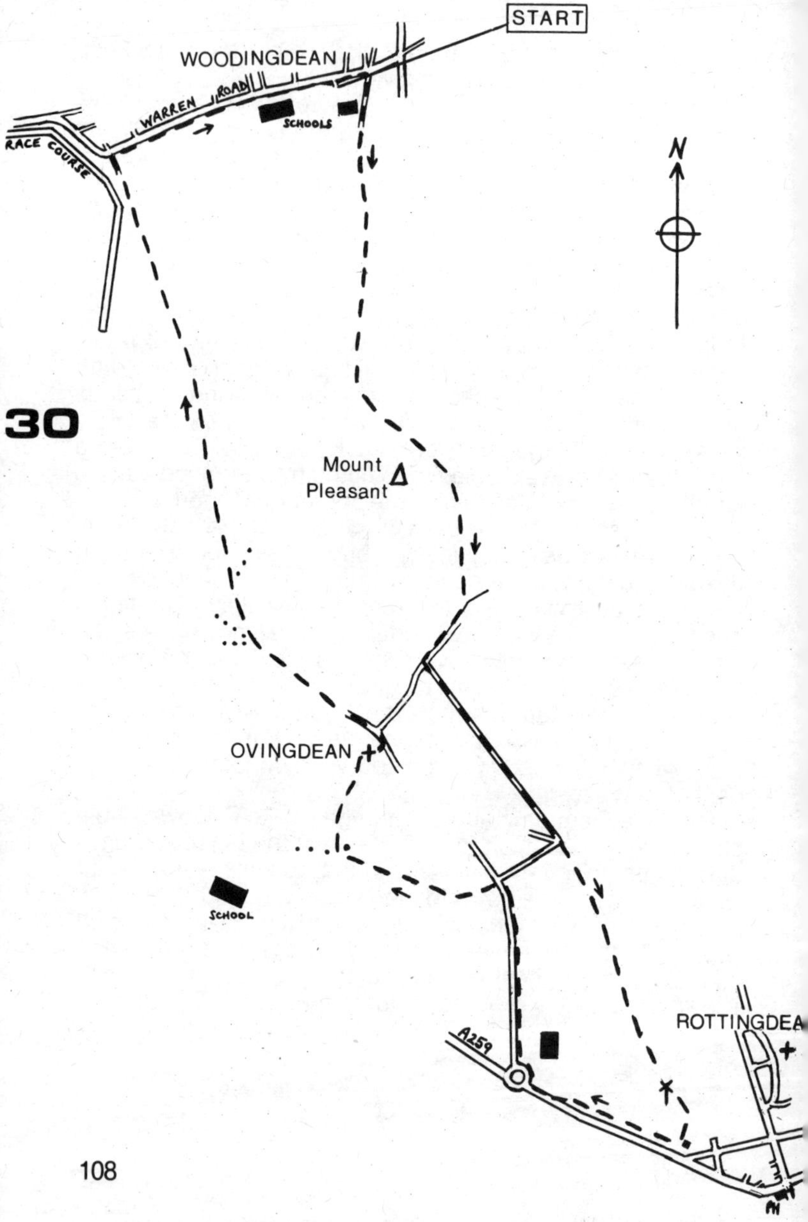
START
WOODINGDEAN
WARREN ROAD
SCHOOLS
RACE COURSE
N
30
Mount Pleasant
OVINGDEAN
SCHOOL
ROTTINGDEA
A259
PH

Walk 30
OVINGDEAN

Woodingdean — Mount Pleasant — Beacon Hill — Rottingdean windmill — Ovingdean — Brighton racecourse — Woodingdean

Distance 6 mls **Climbing** 630 ft **Highest point** 430 ft

Starting point The car park of Woodingdean Community Centre, Warren Road (by kind permission of the Association). Map reference TQ 353057.

An easy walk on gentle gradients, visiting the secluded hamlet of Ovingdean, with a breath of sea air for good measure.

Walk east along Warren Road past the Woodingdean Middle School, and turn R into Old Parish Lane. Passing further school buildings R, continue southward along a broad track which gives a distant view ahead of the windmill at Rottingdean. After skirting the summit of Mount Pleasant, this track joins a made-up road just over a mile from Woodingdean.

Turn R along the path beside the road, which first descends towards Ovingdean village but bears L to go south as Long Hill Road. In just over ½ mile the road takes a R turn, but your way lies straight on, along a downland track which passes just L of the top of Beacon hill, with prominent St Dunstan's on its R side. Once past the summit, descend to the Rottingdean smock mill.

Built in 1802, the mill ground corn for the village until 1881, and now its shell is a landmark, preserved by the local preservation society.

To visit Rottingdean, go past the pitch and putt ticket office and turn L to enter the village by the main road. Your walk resumes along the southern boundary of the golf course, with a distant view to Worthing pier, and a nearer one to the Brighton marina. At the corner of the course, go down the

Ovingdean

path beside a fence to the busy road. If you wish, you may at this point use the subway to visit the beach and undercliff walk.

Resume the walk by taking the footpath going north past St Dunstan's. In about 400 yards, just after passing a bus shelter R, take a footpath L, ascending between fields. Cross a stile half-way up, and continue on the other side of the fence. Look for the circular, brick well-head, where you must turn R to walk north, passing a small wood R before finding a gate in a muddy corner of the field. Go through it and descend beside the flint churchyard wall to Ovingdean church.

Entered beneath a thousand year old yew tree, the church of St Wulstan dates from just after the Norman conquest. It has a heavy, square tower, surmounted by the typical 'Sussex cap', but its chief interior features are 3 graceful arches between the nave and chancel, and a charming little chapel adjoining the chancel.

Leave the churchyard by the eastern lychgate and turn L along the road. When after 20 yards this bears R, go straight on through a farm with large barns. At the next fork bear R into a valley, keeping a golf course L, all the way to the eastern end of the Brighton racecourse. On reaching Warren Road you will notice a fine view of the whole course, including the grandstand, and the TV masted Whitehawk Hill. Now go R along a path beside the road to regain your starting point.

31

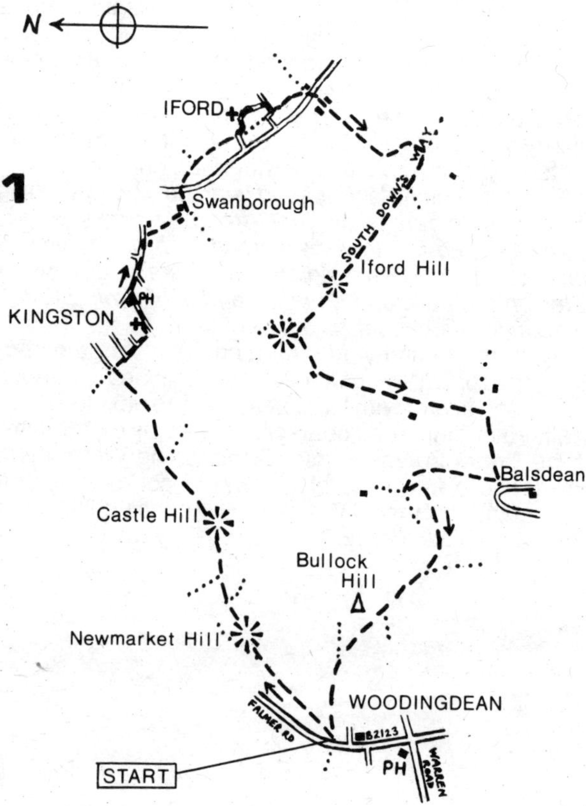
N
IFORD
Swanborough
SOUTH DOWNS WAY
KINGSTON
PH
Iford Hill
Balsdean
Castle Hill
Bullock Hill
Newmarket Hill
WOODINGDEAN
FALMER RD
B2123
PH
WARREN ROAD
START

Walk 31

OUSE VALLEY HAMLETS

Woodingdean — Newmarket Hill — Castle Hill — Kingston-near-Lewes — Swanborough — Iford — Northease Farm — Iford Hill — Swanborough Hill — Balsdean — Bullock Hill — Woodingdean

Distance 11 mls **Climbing** 1300 ft **Highest point** 645 ft

Starting point The rough car parking area in Falmer Road, Woodingdean, about 200 yards north of its junction with Bexhill Road (map reference TQ 356064).

A superb walk on mainly firm ground across some of the unspoiled, rolling downland east of Brighton. There are visits to 2 ancient little churches and spectacular views across the broad valley of the Sussex Ouse.

Take the L of 2 tracks and set off north-east in the direction of the mast near the top of Newmarket Hill, at 645 feet the highest point in the triangle bounded by the Brighton-Lewes road, the Ouse valley and the sea. Walk past the mast and pause near a dewpond R to take in the view.

To the west is Brighton, with the racecourse stands prominent, and beyond it stretches the coastline to Worthing; in the north-west is Hollingbury Hill, and to its R the wooded Stanmer estate, with its mansion and tall-spired church, the widespread buildings of Sussex University and the church of Falmer, with a bold, square tower. North-east are the downs around Lewes, and in the east, only ½ mile away, is Castle Hill, your next target. To the south-east the deep valley called Falmer Bottom leads to Bullock Hill, surmounted by a trig point, and in the distance Seaford Head is guarding the coast.

Continue along the track over Castle Hill, joining the South Downs Way just before the final ascent to the summit. Shortly beyond the top you will notice 3 gorse-filled depressions, one filled with water, near the path to the north-east. Pass them R, and here leave the South Downs Way by going straight on

Iford

downhill in the direction of Lewes, now visible in the valley. Soon Kingston village comes into view below, and your chalky bostal path winds down steeply to enter it. On joining a made-up lane, turn R at once to descend along a bridleway behind the houses. Continue in the same direction when the path becomes 'Church Lane' and again as it passes the tennis courts L. Then follow it L through the trees to arrive at the gate of Kingston church.

Dedicated to St Pancras, this is a small, flint building with a slender west tower. Although much restored, it is unmistakably a 14th century church of the Decorated architectural style.

From the south porch go through a tapsell gate and then L down the village street. Just past the Juggs Arms, turn R along Wellgreen Lane, signposted 'Newhaven'. In ¼ mile find a footpath R which leads over a small rise to Swanborough, giving fine views of the downland peaks R and the Ouse valley L, dominated by Lewes and its Norman castle keep. Walk through Swanborough farm, turn L to pass a Norman manor house and emerge on the Lewes-Newhaven road. Cross the road and a stile on the far side to find the footpath to Iford. Proceed south-east across the corner of a large field, and in 200 yards go through a narrow kissing gate in the fence along the southern side. Now go due south across fields for ¼ mile, negotiating stiles and gates on the way. Arriving on the lane through Iford hamlet, turn L and walk between flint walls and cottages to the parish church.

The church of St Nicholas is mainly a Norman building. It has a central tower with a shingled spire. Within, notice especially the fine decoration on the semicircular arch between the nave and tower, the earliest part of the church.

Go L to continue along the lane through the village for another ¼ mile, turning R at a T-junction. On reaching a sharp R bend, cross a stile ahead and turn L on a path along the east side of a large field. Now proceed south across the middle of this field, and after a further stile, head across the next field to a kissing gate at its far corner. Cross the main road, and set off up a concrete track opposite, into Northease Farm. Pursue this as it heads first to the foot of the downs and then bears L to ascend once more to the South Downs Way. There are good views L to Lewes and the attendant Cliffe Hill and

Mount Caburn, the brook-filled levels around the Ouse and the bulky, bemasted Beddingham Hill.

At the top of the climb pass through a small gate R and walk up the gently rising Way on its high ridge. Beyond a large gate take up a concrete lane continuing over Front Hill and Iford Hill (600 feet), and follow it L when, after a mile, it leaves the South Downs Way to make for a prominent hay-barn. Now unsurfaced, the track immediately swings south along another ridge, with a prospect L to the white cliff of Seaford Head and the towns of Seaford, Newhaven and Peacehaven.

Eventually the bridleway descends towards Rottingdean, and at a fence where the main path turns L, you must go R to continue the descent to Balsdean valley, keeping a fence R. Just beyond the lowest point go through a small gate and turn R on a flinty track towards distant Castle Hill. In about ½ mile you will arrive in a grove, where many paths intersect at the foot of Bullock Hill. Turn sharp L, to ascend at first steeply and then more gently along the top of the ridge called 'The Bostle'. Follow the same track as it veers north-west to pass behind the houses of Woodingdean, with the flat summit of Bullock Hill R. Pass a downland reservoir R, and soon afterwards your path merges with one which has made a longer climb from the grove. Now head west for ¼ mile to regain the parking area by the Falmer Road.

Walk 32
TELSCOMBE

Rottingdean — Balsdean — Pickers Hill — Highdole Hill — Telscombe — Telscombe Tye — Saltdean — Rottingdean

Distance 8 mls **Climbing** 850 ft **Highest point** 410 ft

Starting point The clifftop car park about 150 yards east of the Rottingdean crossroads, on the Newhaven road (map reference TQ 372022).

A truly splendid ramble across rolling downland, on mainly firm ground and gentle gradients. A visit is made to peaceful Telscombe, a secluded hamlet 200 feet up in a downland hollow, and the walk ends with a bracing stretch along the cliff tops and undercliff promenade.

Turn L on leaving the car park, and at the traffic lights turn R to walk up Rottingdean High Street, with its quaint old shops and pubs. Cross Steyning Road, and then go R along Vicarage Lane to pass the attractive village pond and green L. Visit if you can the interesting parish church of St Margaret, a flint building with a Norman nave and Early English chancel and central tower.

After the church, keep walking north for about 300 yards, and turn R up Bazehill Road, which at first rises steeply but soon leads you on to the open downs. Continue along the same lane as it becomes a private road to Balsdean farm and pumping station, and look back for a good view over the Channel and the prominent black smock mill by the pitch and putt course.

Pass the entrance drive to some tile-hung farm houses R, and follow the same tarmac lane, which soon gently descends to the lonely valley of Balsdean. Immediately beyond the point where the road turns 180° to head for the pumping station, take a track L, and in 40 yards go through a small wooden gate R. Now ascend a grassy path between

32

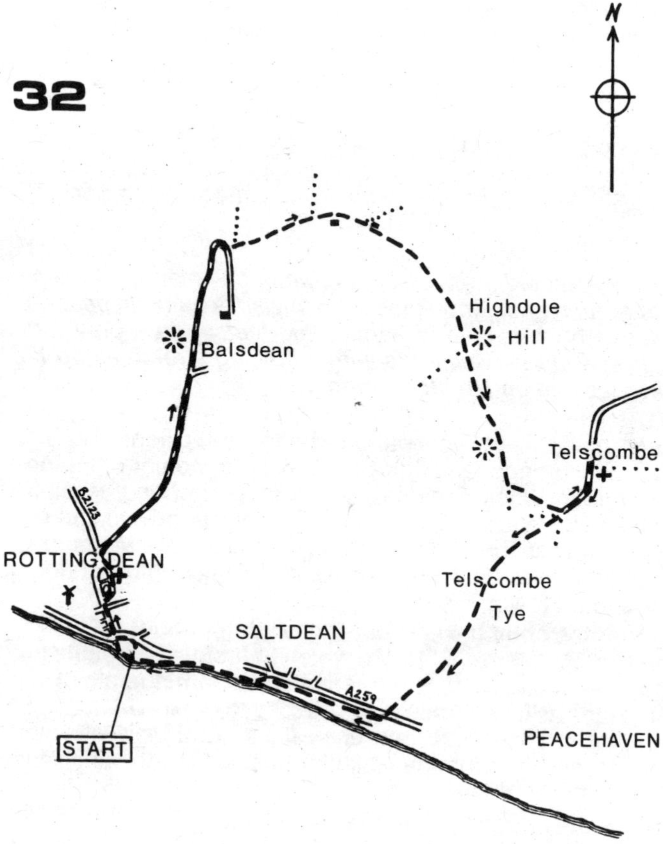

N
Highdole
Hill
Balsdean
Telscombe
B2123
ROTTINGDEAN
Telscombe
Tye
SALTDEAN
A259
START
PEACEHAVEN

fields on the western slopes of Pickers Hill, and go through another gate near the top.

In 200 yards bear R, pass a brick barn R, and in another 100 yards bear R again to pass another barn L. The walk continues south-east for about 1½ miles along a lofty ridge, passing close to the hardly discernable summit of Highdole Hill L and a reservoir R. Notice the fine views, at first R into a valley with Saltdean at its mouth, then L to distant Mount Caburn, Beddingham Hill and Firle Beacon, with Seaford Head farthest south, at the sea's edge. After the first of 2 white houses R of the track, bear L along a bridleway above a deep, wooded coombe. 500 yards later arrive on a made-up lane, turn L along it and descend to Telscombe village.

Telscombe is a tiny hamlet of flint buildings, dominated by the parish church of St Laurence. Most of its fabric dates from the early Norman period, although the simple tower and the north chapel were added about a century later. The interior is dark but has interesting architectural features, including Norman piers and arches. Among other attractive buildings in the coombe are the Stud Farm, whose stables once trained a Grand National winner, the Manor house, the Old Rectory and a row of flint cottages now used as a youth hostel.

Retrace your steps to where you joined the lane into Telscombe. This time, go straight on along a bridlepath over Telscombe Tye. This was one of the ancient sheep downs of Sussex: now registered as common land, it serves as an important green wedge between the modern development at Peacehaven L and Saltdean R.

Walk seawards along this path for just over a mile until it joins the main coast road. Cross it, and walk R along the cliff tops into Saltdean. When the road has nearly reached its lowest point, go L down a path past the toilets and cafe, and finish the walk on the promenade beneath the sheer white cliffs with their streaks of flint. In about ¾ mile, climb the steps R, and you are back in Rottingdean, where there are abundant pubs and cafes. Turn R at the traffic lights to return to the car park.

KEY TO MAPS

route of the walk	hilltop
roads and lanes	windmill
other paths and bridleways	church
railways	other building
triangulation pillar (trig point)	PH public house
hillfort	CH golf club house

METRIC

CONVERSION

CHARTS

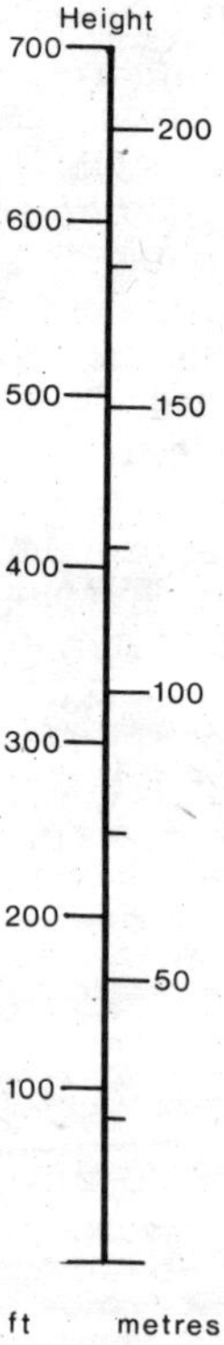

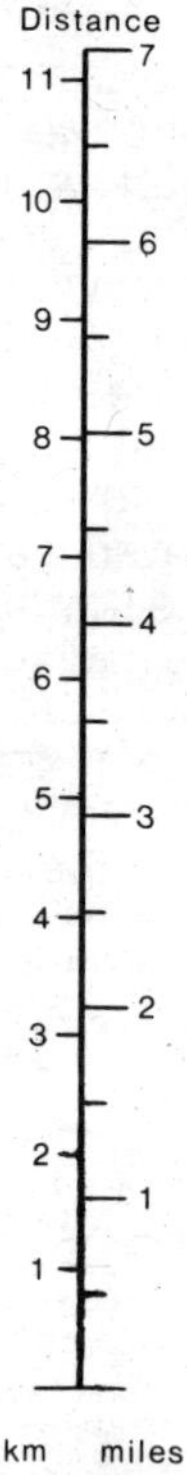